ALIVE

AWAKE

AWARE

Authentic Power through Spirituality

By Christopher A. Pinckley

ISBN-13: 978-0692474075
ISBN-10: 0692474072

Book Design & Formatting
Donna Overall
donnaoverall@bellsouth.net

Gratitude

Thank you to Gil for keeping my head above water through some big waves.

Thank you to Elizabeth and Dan for making it possible for me to incarnate and exist.

Thank you to Shannon for being my beacon of light when the shadows were dark.

Thank you to my friends and family who believed in me and supported my efforts throughout the entire fiasco.

Thank you to an unexpected ally named Donna who helped me to turn this book into something special.

"As a teacher who has had the privilege of sharing personal growth and evolution to millions worldwide, it is easy to recognize a kindred spirit when I meet one. Chris lays out a path to heightened spirituality that is easy to understand and follow for the first time seeker and experienced practitioner alike. He shares his wisdom in a way that makes positive change easy for all to achieve. His authenticity is his greatest gift."

— *Laura Silva, CEO of Silva Life System*

"Chris' work is based on his deep experience and awakening process. It is thought provoking and integral, and covers many important yet often overlooked steps that people must take on the path of awakening. My hope is that it will motivate many people to connect more deeply within themselves and unfold who they truly are."

— *Deborah Rozman, CEO HeartMath Inc.*

"Christopher's timing could not be better. The virtual world is invading every aspect of our lives. Not only do we need a Reality Check, but, definitely, we need to WAKE UP and become AWARE. Very few people have reached a level of awareness that makes them catalysts for other people's transformation. Christopher is one of them. I highly recommend reading this provocative book if you want to Move Up the ladder of awareness."

— *Dr. Clotaire Rapaille, Author of the Bestseller, THE CULTURE CODE, Chairman and CEO of Archetype Discoveries Worldwide*

"*Alive Awake Aware* is a detailed look at the topic of spirituality and consciousness which can help people understand themselves better, and can be used as a guidebook to help the reader discover and wake up on how they want to use spirituality and higher consciousness in their everyday life. It also highlights the workplace and how both men and women need to wake up not only in their personal life but how they create in business. It is when companies, executives, and employees become AWARE that they can impact change that businesses can change for the better. Many company executives do not know that every decision they make, whether they are conscious of it or not has a ripple effect, positive or negative. *Alive Awake Aware* opens the reader to many possibilities that relate to the collective whole, not just one aspect of the human experience."
   —*Nina Boski, Entrepreneur, Movie and TV Producer*

"Another game changer from Pinckley! Sharing his own experiences and the resulting learned-evidence, he deliberately inspires a powerful awakening within the reader creating a bridge to help them integrate into their lives: tips, advice and support on a vast spectrum of topics that demonstrate how to harness the benefits. He shares intimately and first hand helping his readers into a deep dive of self-exploration. Bravo!"
   —*Beatrice Stonebanks, Business Development Specialist and Leader*

"Groundbreaking, powerful, and thought provoking! Pinckley's work will have you redefining spirituality. Read this book only if your desire is to learn what lies at the deepest part of your core."
—*Kathleen O'Keefe-Kanavos, International Bestselling Author, Surviving Cancerland: Intuitive Aspects of Healing, TV and Radio Host: Wicked Housewives on Cape Cod*

"If you're ready to peel back the layers of the onion then look no further. Pinckley has the peeler ready for you; you just need to be ready for what you'll find."
—*Ivan Misner, Founder of BNI and New York Times Bestselling Author*

"A good chunk of my limited amount of time is spent reading and studying anything I can get my hands on to make me better in every conceivable way that I can be. So, I've read a zillion books on self-development and spirituality. I'm going to tell you right now, this book is one of a kind. In fact, you might not be ready for it."
—*Mike Michalowicz, Author of The Toilet Paper Entrepreneur*

"This book challenges the framework of mainstream thinking and culture. A breath of fresh air for someone seeking a new perspective towards a colourful life. A book to get your hands on if you want transformation of self. Grab it and grab your life once again"
—*Jeffrey Slayter, Best Selling Author, Speaker, and Entrepreneur*

"There's only one thing more powerful than thinking, and that's rethinking. Pinckley will have you doing that in this book."

—*Frank Shamrock, MMA Pioneer, UFC/ StrikeForce Legend*

"*Alive Awake Aware* is not just a book but a practical guide to unlocking your true potential by understanding and implementing power of your conscious and unconscious mind, creating healthy boundaries, exploring your spirituality, defining your feminine and masculine energies, practicing authentic communication, and integrating all of the above. A must read for anyone committed to a higher quality of life."

—*Katrina Starzhynskaya, Author, Entrepreneur*

"This remarkable book is a road map to the changing times on our planet. There is no question that we are evolving, and it can be a very confusing time for so many with conflicting teachings about how to approach life, relationships, our spiritual connection, and our livelihood. Christopher has very intentionally and methodically laid out the key areas to focus on, and a fresh and approachable perspective on how to digest each piece without feeling overwhelmed or rushed. This book is going to be a part of my library collection of go-to resources, and required reading for all my clients. Thank you Christopher for creating this priceless gift to humanity."

—*Asha, Spiritual and Business Mentor to Women Entrepreneurs*

"Most people are simply not aware of the power they have to completely transform their own reality. This book will lead you down the pathway to uncover and reclaim your own inherent power through the timeless magic of sheer awareness. Christopher Pinckley's *Alive Awake Aware* is a manifesto that redefines authenticity. Read it, use it, live it."
  —*Gil Alan, Spiritual Luminary, GilAlan.com*

"Combining spiritual philosophies, ancient wisdom, and good old-fashioned practical truths, Christopher Pinckley has crafted a guidebook for anyone on a spiritual or personal growth quest. He opens the narrative reminding us that we are the directors of our own lives by choosing the path of "conscious intention." Then he teaches us how to walk the path as spiritual beings while tapping into our main source of power—our own inner wisdom. As we learn to trust this wisdom, Pinckley reminds us that we have the power to heal ourselves, change our lives, enhance our relationships, and continue to evolve in awareness and compassion, using practical daily routines and strategies that he shares throughout the book."
  —*Barrie Davenport, Author of Peace of Mindfulness and Founder of Live Bold and Bloom*

Table of Contents

Introduction xv
    The Vehicle xviii
Chapter 1 1
  Spirituality: Defining the Indefinable 1
    Spirituality 101 2
    You Are in Control 4
    Spiritual Guidance 5
    Psychics 7
    PhD's 9
    Mind/Body Science 10
    Power Externalization 12
    Your Personal Power 14
Chapter 2 15
  Humble Origins 15
    Unaware Is Only Unaware 16
    Driven 18
    An End to the Tour 19
Chapter 3 21
  The Subconscious Mind 21
    Who You Really Are 22
    Internal Software 22
    Generations of Entrainment 24
Chapter 4 25
  Mass Mind Entrainment 25
    Subconscious Emotional Patterning 26
    Subconscious Beliefs 27
    Generation to Generation 29
    Your Authentic Self 31
Chapter 5 35
  Spiritual Bypass 35
    Unhealed Teachers 37
    Anything Worth Doing 38

Chapter 6. 41
  Mirroring 41
    Participation Is Mandatory. 42
    A Clearer Mirror 44
    Conscious Mirroring 45
    Unconscious Mirroring 47
    Observation Tower. 48
Chapter 7. 51
  Projection. 51
    Belief Projection. 53
    Political Projection: Is There Any Other Kind?. 54
    Parents and Projections 55
    Daily Projection. 57
Chapter 8. 61
  Unconscious Reactivity 61
    The Catalyst. 63
    Stimulus/Response. 64
Chapter 9. 69
  Karma. 69
    Good Things Happen to Bad People! 71
    Reincarnation. 72
    Born Knowing. 73
Chapter 10. 77
  Manifestation 77
    The Law of Attraction 79
    The Integrated Law of Attraction 82
Chapter 11. 85
  The Emotional Body 85
    Access Key. 86
    The Business of Emotion 90
Chapter 12. 93
  Feminine and Masculine Energy 93
Chapter 13. 97
  Relationships 97
    Alone Time 98
    Relationship Energy. 100
    Serial Relationships 102
    Money & Relationships & Empowerment. 103

Chapter 14. 107

Shifting Consciousness. 107

The Speed of Thought 108

Why. 109

How. 112

Chapter 15. 117

Boundary Creation. 117

False Positive 117

Negative Energy Sponge. 119

Creating Space 121

Saying "No" 122

Boundaries for Women 123

Boundaries for Men 124

Loving Yourself 127

Chapter 16. 129

The Spoken Word. 129

Affirming Your Reality 130

The Outer Can Cultivate the Inner 131

What Am I Saying? 133

Speaking with Purpose. 134

Usage and Timing 136

Life Scripting. 138

Chapter 17. 143

Power of the Mind. 143

Nonlinear Thinking. 145

Thought Patterns 146

Chapter 18. 149

Meditation. 149

Techniques. 150

Creating Your Practice 152

There Is No Try 155

Baby Steps 156

Chapter 19. 159

Taking Action. 159

The Integral Path 161

Aligning with Your Goals. 162

Chapter 20. 165
  The Power of Nonattachment 165
    Temporary Transcendence 167
    Constricted Viewpoint. 169
    Consistent Nonattachment 170
Chapter 21. 173
  Expansion vs. Contraction 173
    Expansion 177
    Contraction 177
Chapter 22. 181
  Energy Focusing. 181
    Purposeful Focusing. 184
    What IS Real? 185
Chapter 23. 187
  Creating Authentic Communication 187
    Small Steps. 188
    Creating Space for Authenticity 189
Chapter 24. 193
  The Power of Routine. 193
    High Level Performers 193
    An Innocent Thought 195
    Creating the Routine 196
Chapter 25. 199
  The Integration 199
    Step 1 Acknowledge the Journey 199
    Step 2 Meditation 201
    Step 3 Unplug 202
    Step 4 Observing Unconsciousness. 204
    Step 5 Boundary Creation 207
    Step 6 Mirroring 212
    Step 7 Ceasing Projection. 213
    Step 8 Emotional Integration. 215
    Step 9 Speaking with Power 217
    Step 10 Creating Your Routine. 218

"The Matrix has you." –Morpheus

Introduction

When you are ready to make the profound decision to engage your life's journey with conscious intention then you may begin to become aware of a deeper yearning within you. As you open yourself to becoming more self-aware, which means embodying an inherently higher level of consciousness, you may begin to see a larger picture forming within your mind.

At first, it may seem vague, or perhaps ephemeral in nature, but it is the beginning of your authentic, soul-level calling in life. It's not new; in reality, it has always been there in the back of your mind. It is simply that the mental noise within your *mind* has disallowed you to be aware of its existence until now. Yet, now it is as if a fog has lifted and you are able to finally begin to see that what you have been seeking is actually right in front of you.

Of course, when stated this way, it is a vast over-simplification of a process that can take an entire lifetime. Some people will never know their life's calling. No matter how sad or daunting this may seem, it is the simple truth. It is because discovering your authentic self requires the desire for consciousness to enter into your life on a daily basis, forever.

In other words, this is not a destination; it is a road map. This is a non-ordinary road, which leads to ultimate freedom, achievement, and fulfillment in all ways that can be. However, this road does not lead anywhere external, but rather to a place deep within you, which holds the gateway to your highest potential. It leads inwards to your awakening potential.

The trickiest part of this road could be that it does not reveal itself immediately, even to the devout seeker. This is important to understand so that one does not lose faith along the way. It's tempting to become frustrated or even angry as you engage with this journey to know yourself at the deepest level because the answers you seek usually do not come immediately. Many begin this journey as a means to achieve their goals, only to realize that they must surrender attachment in order to move beyond the realm of the ego.

When this happens, the journey is often given up, and the individual resumes their pursuit of external goals in the attempts to make material gains. Of course, it's important to note that there is nothing wrong with wanting to experience material gain in the world. It is simply that, quite often, this is done at the total expense of the soul-level needs of the individual. When this happens, the happiness of achieving these goals is revealed to be fleeting and insubstantial. In other words, when the soul-level needs remain unmet, happiness remains as a constant pursuit of some means of external validation.

In this way, the individual will move from achievement to achievement, trying to obtain more and more, in hopes that the next achievement will create the internal happiness he or she is craving. Always, though, is revealed the temporal nature of the material world and its pursuits. Again, this is only when it is used as a substitute for unmet soul-level needs. Material gains, when kept in perspective, are a beautiful way to enjoy achievement and contribution in the world. In other words, they need not be demonized or utilized as a scapegoat to deny you fulfillment. You are no less spiritual if you enjoy the material world and its bounty. It's simply making sure that you are not supplanting your inner growth and soul connection with them.

Once you are beyond the need for instant gratification, you can begin the journey in earnest and allow your higher calling to unfold. In the beginning, you may notice that you get vague "ideas" about things that you want to do at some point. You may receive images of ideas or scenarios that are small pieces of a much larger puzzle of something that you will eventually become involved in. Or you may get what some people refer to as "downloads," which means that you'll get a huge block of information in your dream state or perhaps early in the morning upon waking.

Of course, these things could come at any time, but are often more apt to happen when the thinking mind is the least active. This is when your higher nature is able to communicate more directly with you and with less interference from your thinking mind. As you continue on your journey of consciousness, you may become more and more aware of this higher calling as it begins to take shape and form a larger picture. Of course, eventually you will need to begin to take some sort of action to make it become a physical reality.

However, at this level of consciousness, your actions become more guided and thus yield more powerful results. You may still need to move through the feelings of fear, but you will sense that you have a new found depth of power emanating from within you. As a result of this, moving through fear becomes more of an exercise in consciousness and less of an emotional challenge. Whatever you are "called" to do, you will discover that you have a new found strength to meet this calling head on. What may have previously seemed insurmountable to you is now perceived as "doable."

The Vehicle

As you progress along this pathway, allowing consciousness or "authentic power," to build within you, you may also come to another revelation: you have become a vehicle for something greater. At a certain level of consciousness, you become aware that your life is now unfolding naturally and requires little or no force at all. Action is still required, but it is all divinely inspired, which means that every action you take yields a productive and measured result.

In other words, the more in tune you become with spirit, the less you waste energy through any inefficient actions taken. You have become a divine vehicle through which your own spirit can emerge and begin to create massive positive impact upon the planet. As a side effect of this state of consciousness or, perhaps, way of being, your previous experiences of stress or "stressfulness" become supplanted by feelings of inner peace and harmony. At this stage, emotional highs and lows have long since disappeared, and you become more interested in maintaining the subtle feelings of peace and harmony that have begun to grow stronger within you.

Additionally, your life force energy has grown stronger, you feel younger and more vibrant, and your internal power continues to build. You are closing in on what the Vedic Seers purport to be the ability to "harness nature," which means that your intentions are almost all that is needed in order to create your reality. At this level of awareness, your slightest intention has enough harnessing force to move a mountain. Your one, single thought is more powerful than the collective actions of thousands of individuals. You have literally become the change that you seek, and you have done it all by seeking within.

This is the destination; now are you ready for the journey?

Spirituality: Defining the Indefinable

In order to truly understand how and why you do what you do, you must begin to embrace the fact that, underneath it all, you are a spiritual being. In other words, past all of the thoughts, beliefs, and opinions you have about your life and the planet, lies a greater truth. Beyond all over-mentalization or the neurosis of ceaseless thinking lies your authentic nature. Your authentic nature is one of a multidimensional, expanded, boundless, limitless, peaceful, loving, and universally intelligent capacity. This is who you really are.

However, our society has become over-mentalized to the point where we barely give a second thought to anything other than our daily schedule. And when we do take time to honor that deeper yearning to know ourselves, the subject of spirituality has become so convoluted that we quickly get lost in the dizzying maze of teachers, books, and definitions around it.

Therefore, it's important to begin with the concept of spirituality. Understanding what it is will help you to understand its importance and relevance in your life. Without this understanding, it's very difficult to embrace your authentic power.

Otherwise, what are you left with? Are you just a leaf blowing in the wind, at the mercy of the elements, only to one day return to the ground from whence you came? Or, are you something so amazing and so incredibly powerful that, when you realize this truth, it will change your life forever?

I'm telling you that you are this powerful, multi-dimensional, multifaceted, universally connected to all things, being of boundless love and infinite intelligence. However, before you embrace this fact, you must understand the path that lies before you. You must become able to navigate the terrain and understand where your ideals and beliefs came from and why they are not who you are.

Part of this understanding is becoming clear about what spirituality is and is not. Additionally, understanding the different types of teachings and the pros and cons of each will be of great benefit to you. So, allow me to break down this complex subject for you and help you to reveal the truth of who you are.

Spirituality 101

The element of Spirituality that makes it so beautiful is also what can make it rather treacherous at times; it is open to individual interpretation. In fact, spirituality has as many different definitions as there are people on the planet, which puts it at roughly around 7 billion. With so many different definitions floating around, it's no wonder that the topic often seems confusing. If you combine the confusion of individual interpretation with the fact that so many people are searching for meaning within their lives, then you can see the potential hazards.

This means that if one were to write a book and attempt to perpetrate some sort of hard and fast definition of Spirituality or Religion, then they may eventually gain the ability to control people, if this was their desire. And, unfortunately, there have been some who desired this outcome. Luckily, this is the exception and not the norm.

Generally, the information within a spiritual book is relative to the level of self-development and life experience of the author. This means that any time you read a spiritual book, then you are reading information that has come through the filter of the author's own consciousness. It's ironic that often, the more pain and suffering in the author's life, the more likely the material will be of actual value. Of course, this is an overgeneralization, one of many I will make in this book.

In the meantime, luckily for us, there is an over abundance of pain and suffering on this planet which, in turn, has yielded some powerful spiritual teachers and authors over the years. It's also important to note that spirituality does not mean religion. In fact, spirituality supersedes religion because religion without spirituality is nothing. However, spirituality without religion is quite simply the connection to your authentic power.

Religion is a wonderful thing when used as a means to connect the practitioner or devotee with the indwelling spirit within him or her. The impetus for religion was to create a vehicle for this connection to occur on a regular basis. When people gather together en masse with the intention to connect with spirit, then the results can be exponential. In this way, historically, the average person was provided a means to maintain their connection to their own authentic power and, as a result, lead a more fulfilling life.

However, somewhere down the road, almost every religion has been twisted and corrupted by those who seek to wield power over others. Slowly but surely throughout the centuries, religion was remolded into a means of control. Yet, there are those who have maintained the faith and integrity of the various teachings over the years, despite massive amounts of manipulation and corruption. Thus, within each religion, you will still find those who desire to maintain the primary impetus of the creation of religions, which was to help people feel empowered through their own connection to spirit.

However, one must be discerning in whom he or she chooses to put faith in when adhering to any particular doctrine or set of beliefs. If religion is part of your path and you desire to attend regular meetings, then the feeling you will be looking for is one of *empowerment*. Conversely, the feeling that will indicate you may not be in the right place is that of disempowerment, shame, or guilt.

You Are in Control

So, my very first instruction to you is to use your own judgment when reading this or any other spiritual book. Remember that I am speaking from my own life experience, which has been interpreted through my own consciousness filter. You are free to take what works for you and discard the rest.

Now, it's also true that I have completed a certain amount of work on myself over the years and so everything that I speak about is coming from the actual experience of walking the path. In other words, I'm not speaking from theory; I'm speaking from integration. I am speaking as someone who has learned it, applied it, and as a result, altered my own consciousness and destiny with it. This does not mean that I have mastered my own destiny or that I have completed my growth and development. Far from it, I am merely continuing the journey, peeling back the layers of the onion, and striving toward illumination.

In this way, I continue to walk the path just as anyone else would who is seeking self-mastery. Yet, from walking through the fire I have gained something of great and immeasurable value. I have gained access to authentic power. So, although I fully acknowledge my imperfection and the necessity of continued inner work, I speak through the medium of authenticity.

Spiritual Guidance

Perhaps of equal or even greater value is that I have discovered many of the inherent pitfalls when it comes to seeking spiritual teaching and instruction. For instance, one of the most ambiguous, yet potentially powerful types of spiritual guidance is called "channeling." I can tell you from firsthand experience that some individuals who channel, whether they refer to it as their guides, their Higher Self, or whatever they indicate as the source of their information, are powerfully gifted in their ability to provide you with insightful information.

At one point, I worked with a Channel for a couple years, and the guidance that I received always seemed empowering and constructive when I applied it in my life. The cumulative result of this guidance was that my business became more successful, I had fewer ups and downs in my life, and I had more spiritual breakthroughs, which improved the overall quality of my life, as well as enhancing my own connection to spirit.

Yet, despite this positive experience, I've come across a number of channels and channeled books that do not appear to me to be quite as evolved. A negative indicator seems to be the amount of esoteric or ambiguous information in the book you are reading or the guidance you are receiving. I have found with spiritual books that the more esoteric they are in nature, the more likely it is that they will be disempowering for the reader.

The reason for this disempowerment occurs in one of two ways: either through power externalization to the author or entity, or when the reader attempts to follow some sort of abstract set of spiritual exercises in the book that promise miraculous results. These exercises are usually not a form of what I would refer to as mind/body sciences, but are often exercises that are very ephemeral in nature like visualizing angels or calling upon an ancient spirit. Although angels and spirits exist, it's not their job to find you employment or fix your relationship.

So, they were exercises that were not grounded in physical reality or with which you were able to measure any sort of tangible results from engaging with. Of course, much of this experience is subjective to the individual seeker in that some will find value where others do not.

If it is a person who is merely exploring and having fun for his/her own personal entertainment, there is much less potential harm than if it's a desperate individual trying to put his/her life together. For a person who is really seeking to rebuild his/her life and find some meaning, this can be a very dangerous path. This person can begin following the philosophy of the teacher or the book, hoping that it is going to save his/her life. Then, when he or she discovers that nothing has changed, the frustration with life can turn into depression. The reality is that for most people at this level of consciousness, the most empowering thing they can do is to get grounded by taking some physical action-steps to make their life better. In other words, instead of asking for the angels to heal their life, they need to take action to make it better.

It's a thin line between how deeply I value my own channeled experiences with some of the people I have solicited to assist me over the years vs. the inherent dangers of listening to just anybody who refers to themselves as a Channel. Yet, as a result of working with some highly developed practitioners, I have become more connected to my own inner Source. In turn, this has led me to feel as if I am in the process of channeling my own Higher Intelligence more frequently. Thus, my opinion of channeling is that it can be an extremely constructive tool when you trust the source, but can also be incredibly destructive when misused and misunderstood.

Psychics

In the quest to know myself at the deepest level and uncover hidden truths within my subconscious, I've seen just about every type of healer, spiritual teacher, or energy worker that you can. So, in addition to my sessions with channels, I've also seen some psychics over the years. My personal experience is that there is an even sharper line with psychics that distinguishes the difference between those who are evolved and those who are not. The problem with this niche of metaphysical teachers is that it is more glamorized and sensationalized and thus has the propensity to draw a different type of personality to it. This means that, in addition to the authentic spiritual teachers who are naturally gifted psychics and/or those individuals who desire to do the necessary inner work on themselves to become gifted, there are many who want attention, fame, or the ability to wield power over others who are also drawn to this career.

This creates a field packed full of people who refer to themselves as psychics without any real skill or ability. It becomes dangerous when you combine an individual desperate for answers in his/her life with those claiming to be a gifted psychic who are actually drawing from their own unhealed personalities for answers.

Basically, this means that if you really want the services of a psychic, you need to be very discerning with whom you choose to help or assist you with your problems or personal development. Anytime you are hiring someone to tell you something about your life you are in the process of temporarily handing over your power to that person, so it is always a good idea to be mindful. When you engage in this type of interaction, you are also more subconsciously open to suggestion; therefore, you want to be sure you are interacting with someone who is as evolved as possible.

What you don't want is someone who is simply projecting his or her own unhealed version of you onto you. When you are engaging in this type of interaction, you are often seeking the deeper answers to your life and you are psychologically in a more vulnerable state. Most people haven't cultivated enough self-awareness and/or developed and learned how to trust their own intuition at this stage. The end result is that a healthy dose of skepticism will serve you well if you are thinking about hiring a psychic.

There are some evolved psychics who can read the residual energy around you, which means that they can see where the majority of your thoughts lie, and thus advise you on the best course of action to take based upon what you say you want. When this occurs, you can make major leaps in your personal development as a result of inside information about yourself that you were not consciously aware of.

PhD's

Of course, there are also therapists, counselors, and psychologists who work in this field as well. My personal experience is that one needs to be every bit as discerning when seeking the services of any of these types of professionals. Simply because someone has a certain set of credentials by his or her name or degrees that indicate graduation from a prestigious school in no way indicates that person will be good at what they do. In fact, I have often found the converse to be true, which is to say the more degrees and certificates the individual has, the less likely he or she will be able to assist you. Although a gross overgeneralization, the indication here is they will likely have become over-mentalized at the expense of their own emotional body.

Another way of saying this is that they have become ego-identified with their label, degrees, and credentials. In this instance, the likelihood of an authentic connection, which is the primary purpose of a therapist of any kind, is greatly diminished. What this means is that they will be projecting from their own egoic, man-made, textbook labeled, definition of therapy. Interestingly, it also increases the likelihood that you will be returning to them for years and years since they only provide a temporary sense of relief, which occurs when you are in the process of regurgitating your issues. The ego actually enjoys the action of discussing problems because this assures its survival. As long as you are in the process of discussing or mentalizing problems, there is no danger of actually healing them. This is a dance with which the ego is very familiar and happy to engage in.

However, there are more and more "heart-centered" therapists emerging in the world every day. More therapists are awakening to the need to create authentic connections with their patients and thus assist them in the work of healing the neglected emotional body. When a therapist moves from the mind to the heart, she becomes an authentic healer. In other words, this individual considers herself as a healer with a degree.

Most schools that provide PhD programs do not teach how to heal the emotional body, and so it becomes the individual's responsibility to transcend the need for egoic attachment to degrees and labels and become an authentic healer. However, when this does occur, the result is an individual who has gone through many years of schooling to do what he or she loves. This process can yield a highly integrated, professional healer who has the heart-felt desire to be of service.

Mind/Body Science

The reason I began to study spirituality was that I wanted to evolve myself, to learn, grow, and become a better human being. I wanted to understand why I did what I did and, more importantly, learn how to change it. As the years flew by and I continued to read and study spiritual books and texts, I would be drawn back to an inevitable conclusion. It was similar to realizing that you can't reinvent the wheel.

This revelation was that virtually all of the spiritual exercises or techniques that improve the quality of your life were ones that incorporated the mind with the body simultaneously. In other words, it somehow had to combine your mind and your physical body for it to have any lasting and empowering effect upon you or your life.

I found that every time I read a more esoteric style of spiritual book, it often did not contain mind/body exercises or was not grounded in any physical reality. In general, they were mostly philosophy-based teachings with hardly any actual technique incorporated. I came away feeling disempowered and confused almost every time I read one of these books until I eventually got tired of feeling that way and quit reading them.

There is an exception to this rule and occurs when a book is written from a higher level of consciousness and is designed to give the reader what are referred to as "awakening moments" from the mere act of reading the pages. Of course, these books are hard to come by, but a perfect example is Eckhart Tolle's *The Power of Now*. This book has few exercises and could be considered philosophical in nature.

However, for those with enough "cultivated awareness" already, this book can be a gateway to even greater levels of awareness and powerful "ah ha" moments within their lives. Of course, Tolle later came out with the book *Practicing the Power of Now*, which has exercises in it for those who wanted to dive deeper into his philosophy.

The point is that the second book was not needed for those who were able to integrate the consciousness that had been infused into the original work. A few more examples of these types of books are *The Seat of the Soul* by Gary Zukav, *Oneness* by Rasha, *The Teachings of Don Juan* by Carlos Castaneda, and *Power vs. Force* by Dr. David Hawkins. These books can provide potential leaps in your conscious awareness from the mere act of reading them.

Other books that may not have mind/body exercises, yet still have the ability to effect positive changes within your life are those that have real life stories about people who have already made the changes that you desire to make. Although not necessarily a spiritual self-help book, *The Success Principles* by Jack Canfield demonstrates what is possible and, as a result, can entrain your subconscious mind to a higher belief system. Quite often, when the author either speaks from her own real life experience or that of other people, the reader is able to extrapolate immense benefit and even permanently elevate her own consciousness from the mere act of reading the book.

Power Externalization

The biggest pitfall for the spiritual seeker when it comes to chain-reading dozens of spiritual and self-help related books is the potential to completely externalize your power. When you begin to believe that the source of your own personal power lies within someone or something else outside of yourself, then you have begun this process. It can become an addictive process whereby you supplant the necessary action-steps to make any changes in your life with the act of reading book after book, trying program after program, or following guru after guru. This means that you are simultaneously beginning to believe or reinforce the idea that you are helpless to change your life or your life circumstances without outside assistance.

It also means that you have moved from seeking knowledge and inspiration to actually seeking aid. This is dangerous because you may be tempted to start hoping that your life will get better instead of actually engaging in exercises and activities to make it better. The feelings that accompany this state may seem obvious, but you may not necessarily understand why you are suddenly experiencing them: you may feel depression, frustration, sadness, fear, and even apathy.

When you are studying spiritual teachings, whether you are going to a teacher or you are reading a book, and you begin to feel this way, it usually means that you have begun to externalize your power. Additionally, if a book or teacher desires you to give your power over to them, then he or she is not usually of your highest good.

Although I have a great love of spiritual books and books or authors who endeavor to expand the consciousness of the reader, I began to see over the years that it was beneficial to become discerning in what I was reading. Before I had cultivated much awareness and consciousness within myself, I was still vulnerable to the potential to externalize my own power.

Since I knew that I was still seeking, but simultaneously realized that I needed to be discerning, I turned to our innate ability to feel to be my guide in this process. Thus, I started paying attention to how it "felt" to read a particular book or follow a particular teacher. In this way, my feeling power became one of my greatest internal indicators of what I should and should not put my energy into. This process helped me come to the conclusion that some books, teachers, and philosophies seemed less authentic in that they appeared to want to usurp your personal power. They wanted you to look to them for your source of power rather than realize it lies within you.

Your Personal Power

Your Power Source lies only within you and is nowhere else to be found. The ability for you to change yourself and, as a result, change your life lies within you. The catalyst for change lies within you as well. Any teacher, book, coach, guide, or whatever else that you choose to help you to facilitate any change is only a tool for you to help you to unlock your own personal power. They are not the power source, but merely a tool you have chosen to help you unlock your own. On your spiritual journey and road to Self Mastery, this may very well be the single most important concept that you can come away with; *YOU are your own source of Power.*

2

Humble Origins

Another element to add into the equation if you happen to be a spiritual teacher, which I feel is vital now more than ever, is total transparency. With the current proliferation of spiritual teachers and self-help experts that have popped up overnight, it's important for people to know who they are. Are you an authentic teacher who is on the path of awakening consciousness, or are you simply another person attempting to capitalize on pop culture trends? The difference is someone with genuine ability to effect positive change in your life vs. someone who is only seeking power, money, or fame. Thus, in the spirit of transparency I would like to reveal how I became a spiritual teacher and coach.

Everyone who has lived long enough can look back and see how greatly he or she has changed. But, for some of us, those changes are incredible, radical, and life altering, even to the point where you are no longer recognizable as the person you once were. I am someone who fits into this unique category of massive, radical, and cellular level change. The unconsciously reactive, completely unaware person that I was in the first thirty years of my life is mostly alien to me now. Sometimes, memories of this previous life come to me, and they are almost always incomprehensible.

I was born into a very loving but very unaware and un-evolved family. My parents were truly the quintessential "Did the very best that they could" parents. However, my childhood upbringing involved a lot of moving around, being left alone, surviving at the poverty line, being left vulnerable to certain elements, little communication or verbal interaction, little or no self-esteem building, negative reinforcement verbally, a litany of beliefs externalizing the source of all suffering to rich people with money, and some positive reinforcement and demonstrations of love.

In this manner, my childhood was like many others who came from impoverished and uneducated backgrounds. This is to say that, although the past is irrelevant and I no longer identify myself with it, it did have the power to create a unique curriculum for me in this lifetime. After transcending the need to feel as if I was somehow special for what I had been through as well as any potential need to blame my parents for my life circumstances, I was able to see that I had chosen the path of awakening consciousness.

Unaware Is Only Unaware

From the vantage point of a higher level of awareness, I was able to come to two conclusions about my childhood: First, being an unaware or inexperienced parent doesn't mean that you're a bad person rather it just means that you lack awareness. Secondly, a person's beliefs really do create their reality. In other words, my parents, having been very young themselves when they had me, were simply inexperienced in life and completely unaware of how they were unconsciously creating their own reality. They were unaware their behaviors and actions could become imprinted upon the subconscious mind of their child. Simultaneously, they were unaware of how their own subconscious minds, as children, had been imprinted upon by their own parents.

As with most families, no one in ours had ever bothered to stop and examine their behaviors and beliefs or where they came from. No one had ever bothered to ask, "Why do we struggle so much in life?" or "Why is there always so much pain and suffering?" or "Why doesn't anything ever go the way we want?" This can only happen when there is a deep desire within someone to want to know these answers, but most people are preprogrammed to strive only to seek comfort. Self-awareness is something that must be consciously sought after and worked towards in order to achieve.

As a result of this kind of radical upbringing, where sometimes even the mere act of survival could be deemed the goal, I grew up deeply unconsciously. As a child, I was fearful and insecure, but also joyfully oblivious to the insane environments I was placed in. The programming that I received during my childhood began to catch up with me as a teenager and manifest as dysfunctional behaviors. I became fearful of sexuality, fearful of confrontation, and acted out my need for external validation through aggressive attention seeking. I would regularly seek approval by attempting to impress people, but never through authentic connection or communication.

This got me into trouble with school bullies because I would draw them to me through acting out my need for attention. They would zero in on me quickly as a nice target to fulfill their own need for validation. As I got older, I began to work out with weights to try to build a more impressive body to scare away the bullies, but still remained fearful of confrontation emotionally. When I had built a big and impressive enough body, I would even begin to brag about how tough I was while, on the inside, I continued to feel petrified of ever having to actually confront someone.

Later, my unexamined and deeply unconscious programming would lead to seeking approval through other means. I lived my life this way all throughout my twenties by seeking attention and self-validation through weight lifting, alcohol, and women. On the outside, I had built and developed a formidable, attractive physical body and even studied martial arts. On the inside, I was still a scared, undeveloped, unhealed little boy who was abandoned, lost, and seeking attention.

My childhood was not unlike many others whom I knew during this time—it fit a certain unconscious behavioral pattern that deeply ruled my entire existence until I was almost thirty years old. Yet, while I continued to struggle to get my life together, many people I had grown up with were beginning to build lives for themselves. The sharp contrast between me and many of the people I knew served as an added motivational factor that urged me to understand why my life was the way it was.

Driven

During my twenties, I continued to struggle with life as I went from seeking external validation to seeking meaningful achievement to consistently sabotaging myself. What I was not aware of was that I was in a pitched battle with my own massive worthiness issues, which were coming from my subconscious and being acted out unconsciously. This manifested in a variety of ways, one of which was to apply for and secure employment at a job that

I thought might provide meaning to my life. Then, shortly afterwards, I would manage to get myself fired. Then, after an emotional meltdown, I would proceed to repeat the process until, after six or seven years had passed, I had been fired from around fifteen different jobs.

Another way I acted out my subconscious programming was through my rebellion against authority. I never liked the idea of being told what to do, and it manifested through my behavior while driving in my car. In some ways, I was rebelling against mass mind control, which I still feel is valid if you want to protect your subconscious mind from being programmed or brainwashed. Another way of saying this is that, simply because a sign says something, does not mean that you need to create a belief system around it. However, I was racking up speeding tickets left and right and occasionally getting myself thrown in jail. It's one thing to be a rebel, but it's quite another to completely sabotage your own life.

An End to the Tour

Toward the end of my twenties, I finally landed a DUI in Beverly Hills, California. This event seemed to be the catalyst for me to really begin to look at why I was doing what I was doing. I am bypassing quite a lot of difficult learning lessons like creating boundaries by standing up for myself, extracting myself from an endless chain of unconscious relationships, and ceasing the need to subconsciously sabotage myself when I was about to accomplish something meaningful, but this was the beginning of a new era. Shortly after this episode, I began reading self-improvement books, self-help books, and ultimately books about spirituality. The gateway was open, and I was full speed ahead, devouring everything in my path that I thought would help me to understand and improve myself in any way possible. This path would eventually lead to deep introspection, meditation, and redefining who I was and my mission in life. It was the beginning of an authentic existence and hailed a new era of conscious evolution for me.

3

The Subconscious Mind

When you're getting started in this process, the first stop on the road to deciphering why you do what you do should be at the level of the subconscious. It's because this is where virtually all of your programming and beliefs reside. It's important to understand that you are nowhere near realizing how many beliefs you have buried within your subconscious mind. In the beginning, when a person first starts reading and learning about basic spiritual psychology or spirituality, she often overestimates her own understanding of herself. It's easy to do. It's not necessarily step one, but could be step two or three: "Basic awareness leads to false enlightenment" or something along those lines.

The reality is that the first step to tackling the amount of unknown data stored within your subconscious should lead to the realization that "I don't know what I don't know." When you can accept this basic awareness, you can begin to do what I refer to as "the work" in earnest. This means an attitude of humility and respect for the undertaking and sheer magnitude of attempting to walk a path few have the courage to traverse.

It can be daunting to begin to dig through your subconscious programming. Some of the questions that may arise are "What are my core beliefs?" or "Am I a good person?" or "What secret desires do I have?" or "Am I really worthy to be alive?" This may seem extreme, but we all secretly question our worthiness. We fear who we may really be deep inside of ourselves.

Who You Really Are

Because of the fact that, at our core, we are all expanded, multidimensional beings that resonate at the level of unconditional love, you really needn't worry about what you'll find within your subconscious. Sure, it's easy for me to rattle this off as some sort of esoteric or abstract philosophy, but my years of experience and endless studies and, more importantly, life experience indicate that this is a Universal Fact. However, you needn't take my word for it in order to do the work on yourself. After all, another way of labeling this process could be "the ultimate act of self love." A way of saying this is that you don't need labels to begin to seek within and integrate the unhealed emotional patterning that will surface. You only need to want to know yourself at the deepest level.

Internal Software

The subconscious is a lot like computer hardware that runs software programs. The different bits of emotional patterning and the resultant beliefs that were formed during childhood are the programs running within it. It's really as simple as that. You have all of these programs running within your subconscious mind that are controlling the way you think and as a result of that your behaviors. Many of the desires or motivations you have are actually generated by your subconscious. This means that your actions are also controlled by your subconscious. So, a large part of the reason why you do what you do is inauthentic. In other words, it's not something that you want in your heart, but something that you want based upon a program running within your subconscious mind.

If you experience alarm at the idea of this, I would say that it's a healthy reaction. If the truth is that you are operating at around only 7-10% conscious thought, it should scare you. It should scare you more if you want to be free, or worse, if you thought that you were free. In order to be truly free in this world, you must first free yourself from your subconscious programming. This means that you need to find a way to remove or deactivate the subconscious software within you that generates all of your unconscious behavior.

There are a variety of techniques and methods available for those ready to begin the process of deprogramming their subconscious. However, there are really only a few of these that I have uncovered that will actually effect permanent change within your life. In virtually all cases, these techniques and teachings necessitate the commitment to a lifelong daily practice. Most of the claims of instant or rapid transformation are gimmicks that appeal to those who aren't really interested in change, but are definitely interested in bragging rights to claim enlightenment or have something to discuss within their peer group. It may sound a little harsh, but the reality is that in order to alter the quality of your life permanently for the better, then you need to be ready to dedicate yourself to the process.

Generations of Entrainment

It's ironic that it only takes a split second to create a subconscious program that will eventually become a permanent belief and affect you for the rest of your life. However, if you were to step back and view the entire picture, you might be able to see a larger pattern emerge. If you were able to holistically, without attachment, view your parents' beliefs and their parents' beliefs, and perhaps even the parents of your grandparents' beliefs, you might find a striking similarity in behavioral patterns.

This means that, although the impetus of the programs being imprinted into your subconscious by your parents may seem to happen at random or by chance, it is anything but that. Rather, most of your subconscious programs and beliefs will have been handed down from generation to generation. The end result is that it has been an ongoing process for hundreds of years.

This is why extracting yourself from your subconscious programming must become a lifelong pursuit, because in a way you are attempting to battle eons of programming. Additionally, you will most likely be the first in your family to walk this path, which means that it requires an additional amount of inner strength and dedication.

I ask you again: *Do you really want to live the same life over and over again, trapped within a subconscious, predestined prison?* I don't think that you do, and I can and will help you. It's time to "free your mind." So, over the course of this book, I will demonstrate how to create a lifelong practice that will permanently alter your consciousness and lead to the freedom that you long for and richly deserve.

4

Mass Mind Entrainment

One of the foremost experts on subconscious programming, Eldon Taylor, discusses how deeply programmed we have become as a human race by those who wish to control us to behave in certain ways that will assure they stay in positions of power. In his book, *Mind Programming*, he speaks at length about how insidious the subconscious programming has become in the United States alone.

One of his first observations within the book is how this Mass Mind programming starts as early as our elementary school teaching. Eldon says that in the late 1800's the United States, via the powers controlling it, adopted the "Three Tier Education System" from Russia. This system was designed by the Russian Government in the early 1800's to entrain people to become workers who would support the lopsided socioeconomic power structure that placed and maintained only a few people at the top.

The Three Tier Educational System is as follows: Public schools train the worker bees. The worker bees provide labor to power the economic engine. The second tier consists of Private Schools where those who will become assistants to the Elite get their "education."

This is where many of the doctors, lawyers, vice presidents, and CEO's get their training. Then, there is the third tier, which consists of schools most of us don't even know about. This is where the Elite receive their education, training, and networking to maintain their grip on world power. In this way, at a subconscious level, the average person's life has been predetermined before they were even born.

It also makes sense when you look at people like Debbi Fields, Ray Kroc, Henry Ford or Richard Branson who all either dropped out of, or never even saw the inside of a public school. Richard Branson is even quoted as saying something along the lines of, "I shiver to think of what would have happened to me had I stayed on to receive a formal education." These billionaires did not need, nor did they want a formal education, because they were somehow aware at a young age of the potential to be entrained into mass mind, limited thinking.

Subconscious Emotional Patterning

Your subconscious programming starts before you are even born. If you can believe it, you are already picking up and logging things into your subconscious at around six months' development in your mother's womb. The types of programming you are most vulnerable to at this stage are emotional patterning. Your mother's general mood will have a strong impact on your emotional body and precondition you to certain advantages or challenges depending upon what she dwells upon during her pregnancy with you. If she is fearful or anxious, then you will most likely have challenges with fear or anxiety in your life. If she is very happy, then you will have a predisposition towards happiness. If she is fighting with your father often enough, then you may have an undertone of anger in your life and may even associate it with your father or men when you are old enough.

Of course, these are gross over generalizations, but they point to a greater understanding of how you came to be who you are today. More importantly, they can help you to potentially understand some of the reasons of why you do what you do, or feel the way you feel. After you are born, this emotional patterning becomes combined with imagery and continues on until you are probably around five years old. This is why some emotional issues and problems cannot be "psychoanalyzed" at all due to the fact that there is no actual problem to uncover. Rather, there is emotional patterning to be integrated through mind/body sciences.

Subconscious Beliefs

At around the age of five, you begin to both absorb and formulate your own subconscious beliefs about life and living. Many of these beliefs will result from observing interactions between your parents and hearing what they are saying. This type of programming is usually done by association more than by directly adopting an actual belief about something. Your mind has started putting things together like puzzle pieces through the process of trying to make sense of the world. While physical experience is still your number one learning tool, association becomes your number one programming tool. You physically explore your environment and simultaneously hear things being verbalized. Then, your mind puts it all together and associates it with results that formulate beliefs. All of this is done without your conscious awareness, and it predetermines some of the challenges or advantages you will have later in life.

As an example, you may observe your father in a frustrated state while he is at the desk looking through papers. He is talking to someone on the phone, and you overhear the word "bills" a few times. He is clearly negatively emotionally charged with frustration and sadness. If you are young enough, perhaps anywhere between the ages of two and seven, you may integrate this into your subconscious as an association and/or belief. If charged with enough negative emotion from this one observation as a child, you could develop a negative association with bill paying which could lead you to avoid wanting to even look at bills later on in life.

In turn, your subconscious predisposition of wanting to avoid bills, because of the negative emotions that you associate it with, will eventually lead you to experience that exact same feeling. The result is that you will get behind on your own bills because you are avoiding bills due to the fact that you don't want to experience that same emotional pain you did as a child with your father. It's ironic the way in which this subconscious programming, via avoidance behavior, will actually create the very emotional feeling that you are consciously trying to avoid.

Conversely, it's quite possible that you could be a child in that same physical scenario but have a father who is happy to pay bills. He may enjoy paying bills because he is making all the money he needs, which gives him a sense of happiness because he feels that he can adequately take care of his family. If, as a child, you spent enough time around him while he was excitedly paying bills, you may pick up some subconscious programming that will actually aid you later in life in a productive way. In this case, later in life as an adult, rather than fearing bills coming in the mail, you look forward to paying them as it provides a feeling of fulfillment to you subconsciously. As a result of this behavioral pattern, you never get behind on your bills. In turn, this furthers your belief in your ability to pay bills, which serves you in a positive way.

Generation to Generation

The emotional patterning that you receive from your parents is probably the trickiest and most elusive bit of programming which you will ever get. However, the most insidious type of programming is in the form of all of the preprogrammed beliefs that your parents and society at large will pass on to you. As a child, you are inundated with a litany of almost every kind of societal preprogramming that you can possibly imagine. Some of it is helpful such as, "Look both ways before you cross the street." This preprogrammed belief could potentially save your life one day.

However, a belief such as "You need to get a college degree in order to survive" could become limiting. It goes hand in hand with beliefs like "You need a good job" or "You need an education," or "You need to be able to pay your bills," or "You should settle down and get married," or "You need to grow up," and many, many others. These subconscious beliefs, which were preprogrammed into your parents and all of the people around you, are fear-based beliefs, which are designed to entrain you into a system. This system is the "Mass Mind" and feeds off of fear and suffering.

You may be thinking, "Well how does a college degree lead to suffering?" A college degree does not, of itself, lead to suffering. However, being entrained into the mass mind leads to the subversion of your authentic self, which is your true nature. In other words, all of this entrainment through mass mind beliefs can and will turn you into a worker robot. Even then, it's not all bad as there are plenty of people who lead very happy lives through this mass mind entrainment. For many people, ignorance is bliss. They are not ready to awaken to the concept of "independent thought" just yet. Although they are actually playing a role as a very small "cog" in the wheels of the giant mass mind engine, they often feel the contentment of living within the "comfort zone." This contentment will last as long as they are able to maintain the comfort zone lifestyle.

However, as soon as an event occurs that demonstrates just how powerless they truly are, they may awaken to the realization that they are actually not free. As long as you are looking to an outside source to take care of you, you will remain entrained to the system and the powers that are controlling it.

Of course, simply pursuing a career that requires one or more degrees does not, of itself, indicate that you are entrained into the system. It is entirely possible for you to have an authentic desire to receive a formal education and remain an independent thinker simultaneously. It is simply that, when plugging into the formal education system, you put yourself at risk of mass mind entrainment.

Another way of saying this is that you are putting your subconscious mind at risk of becoming entrained into a system of thought that is designed to create a dependency. This is why, if you are someone who strongly simultaneously desires both freedom of thought and a formal education, it is best to pursue attendance at the most progressive, leading edge school that you can. Doing this will increase the potential for innovation and decrease the likelihood of subconscious entrainment.

As you begin to become more aware and elevate your consciousness, you will inevitably also become more aware of how deeply you have become "programmed." In turn, this will yield the awareness of how deeply the people around you have become programmed as well. It's tempting to judge others whom you may observe as this revelation begins to dawn upon you, and yet, this only leads to becoming emotionally charged to certain people and situations. Instead of pointing fingers and laying blame, realizing that the world is perfect just the way it is will serve you well on your road to enlightenment and awareness. Another way of saying this is that, in order for you to have a positive impact upon the world and its people, the most powerful thing you can possibly do is to continue doing the work on yourself.

Your Authentic Self

As you continue to observe and become aware of how prolific the mass mind programming is in this world, then you may come to an even more profound revelation. This is the revelation that, even seemingly helpful and innocent beliefs like "Look both ways before you cross the street" are actually forms of entrainment in themselves. Another way of saying this is that we have this amazing and powerful authentic nature within ourselves that we are all born with. However, almost as soon as we pop out of the womb, we become inundated with artificial beliefs to the point where our authentic nature is subdued and completely covered up. In essence, what this means is that we become dependent upon mass mind beliefs because we are trained to ignore and mistrust our own intuitive nature.

In small ways, we have all experienced this phenomenon in one form or another. As an example, I remember the experience of learning to drive with my dad when I was almost seventeen. Although he had the best of intentions, he was not the best teacher. His version of teaching me how to drive was to nervously watch my every move to the point where I felt as if he were going to dive into my seat and take over at any second. This energy was so pervasive and domineering that, for many years afterwards, all it would take was for any person in the passenger seat to begin behaving like my father in order to have an adverse effect upon me.

So if someone who had control issues like my father was in the passenger seat while I was driving and felt the need to double check my every turn and lane change, I would revert back to my subconscious entrainment from that time period with my father. I would begin to second guess myself, get nervous, and even sometimes wait for approval from the passenger before making the turn or lane change.

In a weird twist, an additional facet to this entrainment is that we also have the tendency to perpetrate the other end of the entrained behavior as well. So, another unconscious behavior that I enacted for many years before I became aware that I was doing it was to try to control the behavior of the driver when I was the passenger.

However, this is referred as "projection" which means trying to make your truth into someone else's. This meant that I would become the fearful one who needed to attempt to control the driver because I did not trust that I was either safe or that the driver was fully capable. It's interesting that, in essence, you become as helpless in this situation as the person you are trying to control. You are unconsciously compelled to act and behave in this way due to subconscious entrainment. "Awareness" of the unconscious or entrained behavior is only the first step. Simply because you have become aware of one of your subconscious beliefs or behaviors does not necessarily heal, release, or integrate it. Awareness, by itself, does have the power to heal the behavior or issue within you. However, more often than not, you will need to move beyond the act of awareness and into the process of awakening. Awakening, then, is the journey that we all must take at one point or another.

5

Spiritual Bypass

Before going too much further into subjects like "projection" or "unconsciousness," there is a need to address an important and extremely relevant aspect of spiritual self-help. To reiterate, there is a plethora of information and, unfortunately, misinformation available for the masses to read, study, and digest. One unfortunate byproduct of this mass of materials is referred to as the act of making the "spiritual bypass." What this means is that the reader, studier, or seeker begins to turn to spirituality as a means of escapism from their physical reality.

Thus, instead of facing their physical reality or, more importantly, facing and confronting a valuable life lesson which they can learn and grow from, the seeker is able to escape into spirituality as a means of avoidance. Further, upon following some of these books and practices, the reader may even begin to self-validate or rationalize their choice not to confront the physical reality of their life. In this manner, one can begin to utilize many of the philosophies or ideologies that they study as a means to attempt a bypass of their physical life lessons.

You may ask, "Well, why is that a bad thing?" The reason this often proves to be harmful to seekers is that they avoid confronting their own fear or anger. So, rather than challenging themselves to face and confront a fearful situation that could be the potential catalyst for growth and expansion, they retreat into their spiritual practice or philosophy. Examples of things people can bypass could be standing up to a co-worker who is bullying them, applying for a new job which offers greater pay and more responsibility, asking out their dream partner on a date, learning a challenging hobby like flying or skydiving or scuba diving, traveling abroad to a new country, auditioning for their dream role, displaying their artwork for others to see, moving to the city they've always dreamed of, speaking in front of a group of people, starting their own business, and the list goes on.

For some of you reading this, many of these examples may seem easy enough. You may even be thinking to yourself, "Why would I not want to do these things?" If you have a strong enough fear of something then, subconsciously, you may begin to try to find ways to avoid confronting that fear. In general, this is true for all people, but every person fears something different. Unfortunately, spirituality often becomes the scapegoat for many who want to find a reason to not have to move through their fear or anger. The avoidance of anger is also fear-based in that it is usually a fear of your own anger or anger at yourself for not doing the things that you want to do in your life.

The end result of someone who rationalizes not living the life of his dreams through spirituality is usually either a deep-seated discontentment with life or a neurotic need to convince everyone else of his beliefs. On the one hand, you have a person who begins to demonize his desires and project negative judgments onto people who are doing what he secretly covets and want to experience within his own life. On the other hand, you have someone who is deeply unconscious and feels the compulsive need to convince everyone else to believe as they do in order to self-validate their own path.

Of course, in both instances, a healthy lifestyle is not sustainable for long. Eventually, the envy that the person feels is too much to bear and his life begins to contract around him. They move from envy and frustration into depression because they are denying themselves the much-needed fulfillment of working through physical life lessons. They may even begin to feel bitter toward other people who are doing what they want to do in life and make passive-aggressive attacks. The individual may even attempt to physically remove himself from certain environments so that he can feel better. The problem is that, wherever you go, there you are. There is no permanently avoiding physical life lessons; there is only indefinitely avoiding them.

Unhealed Teachers

Another problem created by the spiritual bypass is the plethora of unhealed "spiritual teachers" who have also used spirituality as a means to completely avoid confronting fear. Many lost spiritual seekers will wind up in the emotional nets cast by these unhealed teachers in attempts to make sense out of their lives. Now, the problem is compounded because here is an individual who is professing to be an authority and is ready and willing to validate your physical fear of life through escapism into spirituality. Now, instead of learning to stake your claim in the world and move through your fears, you are told that angels are healing you. Instead of building up the courage to ask your dream partner out on a date, you are told that he is "Waiting for the right time to present himself to you." Instead of developing and elevating your consciousness by integrating suppressed emotional charges from childhood, you are advised that you are special, and this is why your life is so hard. Instead of taking action steps to get out there and create the life of your dreams, you are told to simply visualize it, and it will be so.

Again, I am making some vast overgeneralizations. However, any time you avoid moving through fear, you are actually trading a small amount of pain for a larger one. And the larger one is the one that stays with you and continues to grow and create more pain and suffering for you over the years. This pain will never go away until you confront it through physical action-steps to work through it or mind/body sciences to integrate it.

Anything Worth Doing

You may be wondering then, "How do I discern between good and bad spiritual teachers?" First, I will take you back to the fact that you are your own center of power. Your power and your intuition both lie within you. If you are really seeking a spiritual teacher, first tap into your intuition about it. Ask, "What do I need?" And then give yourself some time to see where you may be guided. Next, you may wish to follow the age-old adage of, "Don't look for your husband in a bar."

Another way of looking at this is that you will not likely find the best array of spiritual teachers located in booths at the fair. You may also wish to avoid anyone who is making promises of instant transformation. There is nothing instant about spiritual growth and evolution. It is a journey that lasts a lifetime, and some may even argue it lasts many lifetimes. A spiritual teacher is different from a pop-culture phenomenon in that he is usually teaching you a "practice" which you will do over your entire lifetime. If, after you have attempted to tap into your intuition about it, you have still not discovered or been "led to" a good teacher, then physical research becomes your best tool. It may take some time and willingness to experiment, but eventually you will find the right teachers and books to start your journey.

Is it actually possible to make radical transformations in short periods of time? The answer is absolutely, "Yes!" However, in general these radical transformations do not happen according to your intention, but rather as a result of your continued efforts and dedication to the path. Sometimes, exposure to a powerful teacher, guide, or coach can become a catalyst which seemingly catapults you into a much higher level of consciousness in a relatively short amount of time.

However, when this occurs, it is usually because you were ready for it, and the teacher, guide, or coach was merely just that, a catalyst. If you are not truly ready to jump ahead, then there is nothing you can do to make it happen. You must confront your fears and begin to cultivate awareness through the daily practice of some form of mind/body science. A good teacher can help you to keep the course with his or her presence, but cannot substitute doing the inner work that you will need to engage with on your own.

6

Mirroring

A challenging and yet necessary step in the evolution of your consciousness is coming to the profound revelation that everyone and everything in your physical life experience is merely an outer reflection of what you are holding onto internally within your psyche. When you come to this step in the evolution of your consciousness, then your awareness takes on an intricate series of awakening moments that will lead you to some startling ramifications. The most powerful of these ramifications is that you are the true creator of your own life experience.

This means that all of the beliefs and emotional patterning which have been programmed into your subconscious act as the baseline upon which you create your reality. Your consciousness then projects all of these beliefs and preconceived ideas out onto the matrix of people, places, and events around you. In turn, all of these people, places, and events begin to take on the stories that you give them and behave according to how you believe they will. Since this is all happening at a level of consciousness that you are unaware of, you are not aware that it is you who is creating it.

At first glance, this may seem to be farfetched and unrealistic, or perhaps even "woo-woo." At this point, you may be thinking that I have overstepped my bounds and you are going to put this book down. And yet, in the back of your mind, is the suspicion that I am absolutely correct. You suspect this to be true due to the curious tendency of people to behave and do things in your life that you "just knew" they were going to do. It almost feels as if you can predict the behavior of the people around you on a consistent basis. Is this because you are incredibly intuitive or psychic?

Or, is there something else, slightly more insidious going on here? Believe me when I say that one of the most freeing and enlightening facets of elevating your consciousness is arriving at the level of awareness where you can begin to "see" how you are eliciting certain responses from people unconsciously.

Participation Is Mandatory

You are always participating in the act of "mirroring" unconsciously. It's similar to knowing that you are the creator of your own reality although this is only one facet. *Do you create all of the people around you?* No, of course you don't. However, you do create your own personal version of them in your own reality. This is why you can have two people describe the same person completely differently. "That's weird; Tom is always really nice to me!" How many times has this happened in your life? A situation where you discover that other people admire a person you really dislike.

Or, perhaps the opposite, where you really enjoy being around a person that other people seem to really dislike. This occurs because each person is reflecting her own consciousness onto the world around her, and no two people will ever see the world exactly the same.

This is especially true with humans because we unconsciously elicit certain responses from other people's unconsciousness to "role play" with us according to our beliefs and stories. This means that you energetically engage a person before you actually physically engage him. Your subconscious mind has an entire story about someone, with varying beliefs, roles, and labels that are automatically assigned if you are deeply unconscious. The other person has the same internal process, simultaneously occurring within his subconscious, unconsciously. The two of you engage in an unconscious role-play that is completely inauthentic.

In other words, it is completely preconceived, and there is no hope of creating authentic communication. This is yet another reason why it is vitally important to elevate your consciousness so that you can create authentic communication with other people. Authentically communicating is infinitely more rewarding since there is a deep feeling of fulfillment that accompanies this type of interaction. You also feel more centered and at peace when speaking authentically with another person. This is because, at this deeper level of communication, which we refer to as authentic, there is less neurotic projection and more emotional honesty.

It is also important to remember that emotional honesty is not the same thing as emotional projection, which is also a version of emotional dumping. Rather, emotional honesty is when someone lowers their guard enough to tell you what they are really, truly feeling. Currently, this level of consciousness in communication is very rare. Part of the reason for this is that both parties must be able to participate otherwise the unconscious person will project their unhealed emotional issues and beliefs onto the emotionally honest person. This means that, instead of honoring this profound and extremely rare moment where someone is sharing her authentic truth with you, you aren't really listening, but simply waiting for an opportunity to tell her how to fix her life or to extract even more information from her to unconsciously leverage it over her. This means that her problems are now feeding your ego instead of your soul.

Or, in another instance, it can mistakenly be taken as a sign of weakness when the reality is that the ability to be emotionally honest is a sign of strength. This means the person who is listening to you will begin to act in a patronizing manner as if they are somehow elevated beyond your small problems.

A Clearer Mirror

What's important to note is that, as you elevate your consciousness, your view of people and the world becomes more "uniform." You begin to see the good in all people, places, and events. It's not that you are trying to force yourself to see the good in everyone, but rather that it begins to occur naturally on its own.

Conversely, if you are around someone who has elevated her own consciousness, you will most likely notice the "lighter" feeling which you get from spending time in close proximity to her. In fact, you may begin to feel drawn to her more and more. This is because you unconsciously sense the "free" feeling you get from being around this person. What you are actually free from in this instance is yourself. Rather, you are free from your own unhealed projection of the world when you are in this person's presence. This is why when an enlightened sage emerges, people begin to flock to his or her presence. Unconsciously, people sense the freedom that they have longed for.

Additionally, it's why spending time in Nature is so powerful. In Nature, you are also free from projections. The forest and the trees will absorb your unconscious, negative beliefs and unhealed emotional projection without mirroring them back to you. It is the same with spending time at the Ocean or in the Desert. Here also you are free from yourself. You are free from the repercussions of your own negative perception of the world that you project outwards onto it. Whether in Nature, the Ocean, or the Desert, you will feel more at peace than you normally do as a result of the lack of reflective stimuli mirroring yourself back to you. It's as if your consciousness is finally free to just "be."

Conscious Mirroring

Mirroring with people can occur both consciously and unconsciously. There are some companies who train their sales people to purposefully mirror the customer's behavior. In fact, many telemarketing firms will instruct their employees to mirror the accent of the potential customer on the other end of the line to the best of their ability. You may be wondering why a company would want to do that. It's because, at a subconscious level, the intended recipient of the sales call begins to feel more comfortable. The subconscious operates on the basic principle of keeping you safe in your comfort zone. So, when someone sounds and acts like you do, subconsciously you feel as if they must be a safe person to be around.

The end result is that, the more comfortable a company can make their potential prospect, the more likely they will be able to sell them a product or service. This is an example of "conscious mirroring" where a company purposefully uses a basic, subconscious familiarity trick to get their potential target to lower his or her guard and make a purchase. On a subconscious level it's like saying, "Hey, I'm just like you, which means you can trust me!" You may be thinking this seems "insidious," but there are far more insidious techniques and tactics at play in our consumer world than this.

Another way you may consciously mirror someone is with physical boundaries. You may sense that the person you are standing across from does not like people to be too physically close to him or her. Sensing this, you may purposefully keep your distance to honor this invisible boundary that you non-physically sense. In this way, you are demonstrating respect for this person's comfort level concerning physical closeness. It's an entirely different subject to discover whether this person has consciously or unconsciously created this boundary.

Is this person aware that he or she is uncomfortable with the physical closeness of other people, or does that person unconsciously react with body language and emotion when someone gets too close? Is this person conscious or unconscious about this choice? Usually, most people are unconscious of their choices until they make the decision to begin the journey towards awareness.

Unconscious Mirroring

The vast majority of people mirror each other unconsciously. Perhaps the most important aspect of unconscious mirroring for the conscious seeker is beginning to see that everyone around you is mirroring a different facet of you. This means that all the people in your life are mirroring different facets of your psyche back to you perfectly. The closer they are to you in emotional connectedness generally means the more they will be mirroring back to you a part of yourself. Thus, the casual acquaintance may be lightly mirroring back to you a small part of your psyche, whereas your mate or life partner may be mirroring back to you the dominant facet of your psyche.

At first glance many people have great resistance to this concept and think "What, he is nothing like me!" or "I am nothing like that person, that person is despicable!" This occurs when another person is mirroring back to you a part of you that you are deeply unconscious of. In other words, when you have a deeply unhealed facet of your personality that is totally unconscious, you will not wish to acknowledge it. You will be tempted to keep asking: *How could that person possibly represent a part of me?*

The more deeply unconscious you are, the more likely that you will continue to externalize blame for this other person's behavior and mannerisms back onto him when they are in the process of interacting with you. In fact, it is not until a much higher level of consciousness is achieved that you can be expected to take responsibility for the way in which everyone around you is mirroring back to you a part of yourself. Deeply unconscious individuals will continue to rebel against the people in their lives that they do not like, all the while not understanding that they are actually rebelling against a part of themselves.

Observation Tower

Of course, the answer to all issues within your life is through the elevation of your consciousness. In this instance, a way to begin the process of becoming aware of yourself is by observing the people you interact with. What do they do that you like about them? What do they do that you can barely tolerate? Take some time to just "be" with these things for a while. Upon meditation on these behaviors, see if you can become aware of ways that you perpetrate both types of behaviors in your own life. If you take enough time to meditate on it, you will inevitably see how you emulate both the behaviors that you enjoy as well as the ones that you dislike in others. Through this process, you can begin to bring areas of your psyche that you are unconscious of into the light of consciousness.

Of course, this is more so through the process of examining the behaviors of individuals whom we have strong resistance to. We are more unconscious of how we elicit behaviors from people that we cannot tolerate or whom we have long-standing issues with. This does not imply that you should tolerate someone who is abusive to you, though. Rather, in some instances, it is best to first extract yourself from the situation physically. After the fact, the power of reflection and meditation upon how this person represents a part of you can be extremely empowering. At the very least, it may help you to discontinue a destructive behavioral cycle. At the most, it will lead you to the integration of a part of your psyche and permanently augment your consciousness.

This profound level of awareness should be approached one step at a time. You can begin by observing the people you interact with in the beginning. Then, you may begin to inquire within yourself as to how you may be like some of the people you are observing. Then later, you may be startled to suddenly become aware of the fact that many of the behaviors, which you do not enjoy in others, are behaviors that you, yourself, may perpetrate unconsciously. Now you can take the step of beginning to shift your own behaviors and watch as the outer changes you make begin to reflect a new inner shift within your psyche. This means that you have just elevated your consciousness and become more powerful.

7

Projection

The act of mirroring happens through the process of "projection." During this process, people unconsciously project their own versions of each other onto each other. At a base level of consciousness, this happens continually with every single person you interact with. This is the level of consciousness where you unconsciously create all of the other person's ideals, beliefs, and preconceptions, by projecting them from your own subconscious. You determine how they are going to behave and if they will like or dislike you.

As an example, you may have the subconscious desire to prove yourself to certain types of people. So, when you encounter someone who fits the criteria and emotionally triggers you in this way, you begin to unconsciously enact behaviors that are designed to get that person to like you.

However, to this other person, your attempts to get him/ her to approve of you are abrasive and alienating behaviors. This other person feels as if you are over-eager and does not like your attempts to win them over. When he encounters you, his unconscious story is that you are a "pleaser." So, the more you attempt to unconsciously win his favor, the more he will unconsciously try to distance himself from you. Each time you encounter this person, or someone who represents this person to you at an unconscious level, you will both engage in unconscious role-play that ultimately reinforces your subconscious beliefs. Additionally, there is a magnetic quality that your emotional fields produce which draws you to each other. This field grows stronger as you build upon the emotional charge inside of you that is creating it. It's interesting how, the more you try to gain approval in this manner, the more you alienate people from you. When deeply unconscious, this building energy field will keep both parties coming back for more.

If a particular issue is strong enough for you then, when in a crowd of people, you will inevitably draw this one single person to you out of the entire crowd. It can be maddening for you and seem as if you cannot escape it. The reality is that you can't actually escape the issue because the issue is within you. In other words, you are carrying this projection around with you, and it will be there until you resolve it through awareness or some form of mind/body science. No matter where you go, you will still carry around the unresolved emotional charges inside of you that will inevitably activate the corresponding dormant charges within another person who resonates on the level of the issue.

It's like the little boy who begs his mom to put him in another school so he can get away from all the bullies in his current one. If his mom relents and puts him in a new school, he may be horrified to discover there is the exact same number of bullies in the new school. This is because he has brought his fear-based projection with him and unconsciously recreated the same scenario at the new school. Some people may be tempted to think, "How could a little boy possibly be made to feel responsible for being bullied at school?" It may sound harsh or indifferent, but it is the reality. It does not mean that there is any justification for bullying by any means. Rather, it means that we are all responsible for the emotional charges that we carry around and project out onto the people around us. In this instance, there are many possibilities, but one is that he will need to learn to stand up for himself. When he does, his life will improve in ways that he currently could not imagine.

In fact, once he conquers this fear, as an adult he may go on to pass legislation later in life that will improve the quality of public schools. It could be his life path to create a new type of school system that will empower children to feel worthy to stand up for themselves and not be bullied. *Who knows?* The point is that; we don't.

Belief Projection

The most common form of projection that people refer to when discussing the topic of projection is "belief-based projection." This is the type of projection where you attempt to make your truth into someone else's. It is the most easily understood form of projection. At its deepest level, we are all projecting our own version of reality out onto the world and each other to create our own life experience. However, at the surface level, we utilize an inner and understood "should" to attempt to get other people to fit into our version of reality based upon our own subconscious beliefs.

As an example, some people feel that when you are in traffic you should stop or slow down to let someone into the lane in front of you when a person puts on his/her turn signal. However, there are plenty of other people in the world who feel that, simply because you put on your turn signal, it does not give you the right to "cut them off." One group feels that you should be polite. The other group feels that you should be respectful. *So, who is right?* Unfortunately, or perhaps fortunately, there is no way to tell who is right. The only way to discern anything is by being more in touch with your intuition about what feels "right" or "wrong" to you. The more you elevate your consciousness, the more you can begin to co-create your reality in cohesion with the people around you. Instead of "me vs. you," it becomes "us creating together." However, human beings are still a way off from creating their reality in this manner, so the very best you can do is to elevate your own consciousness and allow your energy to affect other people in a positive way.

Political Projection: Is There Any Other Kind?

As a population, we are constantly projecting our beliefs or our version of right and wrong out onto all of the other people around us. The greatest separation or excuse for separation that we have ever created is politics. This is where the greatest amount of projection about the concept of "right and wrong" takes place. Every political opinion, position, system of thought, or ideology is heavily laced with an underlying "should." Nothing is ever based upon the highest or greatest good for all concerned. Rather, it is almost always about one group attempting to get another group to comply with their system of thought. Each group attempts to project its "correct" version of reality onto the other, all the while creating greater and greater separation through the building of resistance to each other.

Politics is so deeply entrained within our subconscious programming that we will often foam at the mouth in a fit of rage to defend our positionality. In this regard, we will defend our version of reality to the death at the least and, at the most, will attempt to bend the wills of others to adhere to our projection. It is the greatest and longest standing projection that we have ever created and forms the basis for all separation in the world.

The problem is not that we have differing beliefs about life and the nature of reality. The problem is when we try to make our truth into other people's truths. When you project your truth onto another person you are, in essence, committing an aggressive act against that person. You are saying, "You need to adhere to my version of reality." Additionally, you are usually back-ending it with an understood "for your own good."

Parents and Projections

Even well intentioned parents struggle with this concept. It's one thing to warn your children about the dangers of fire. It's quite another to attempt to instill within them a life-long, deep-seated fear of anything flammable. Warning your child to be careful that they could burn themselves on the stove may seem prudent.

However, telling them over and over again to stay away from matches, candles, ovens, gas burners, and light sockets could be potentially damaging. Now, instead of educating or sharing information with your children, you are projecting your own traumatic fear of fire onto them. In turn, when they are old enough to have their own children, not only will they have to deal with a subconscious fear of fire as an adult, but they will also project this subconscious fear onto their children.

Some of you may be tempted to ask, "Well, why is it so

bad to warn your children about fire?" I am not saying that it's bad to protect your children from burning themselves at all. However, I am saying that you can create some seriously limiting beliefs for your children when you project your own unhealed, unaddressed emotional issues onto them. This is why it is always better to "share" information with your children than it is to drill it into them.

Thus, a better way to help your child avoid being burned might be something along the lines of, "Hey, I just want to let you know that if you play with fire or touch the stove, that you could burn yourself and it will be painful." Of course, some children are more rambunctious and not as easy to instruct. So, some of you will be thinking "That's easy for you to say, but you don't know little Johnny!" True enough, sometimes the only thing that will suffice is the actual experience. In fact, for some children, there doesn't seem to be any satisfaction until they learn for themselves. Since you cannot put these little foragers in cages, nor would you want to, you may have to accept that they will want to experience certain things for themselves.

However, if you were to adopt this new model of "sharing" with your children rather than "telling" them, you might come up against the projections of other parents you know. "You're doing what?" might be the response that you get from your neighbor across the street when you explain your radical new approach to parenting. It will most likely be followed up with something along the lines of, "You really shouldn't do that," or "You really should be more direct with your children," or "No, you need to tell them what to do." If they are on a slightly higher level of consciousness, they may ask, "Oh really, how is that working for you?" And, an even slightly higher level of consciousness might elicit the response "Oh, that's interesting." This means that if you decide to expose your conscious and unorthodox method of parenting to other people, then the responses may be more reactive if they are less developed.

Daily Projection

The higher the level of consciousness of individuals then, not only are they less projective, but additionally they're less reactive. An interesting side effect is that you can safely share your ideas with these types of people because you know they are not going to react and judge you for them. In the meantime, as you begin to mentally process the subject of projection, you may begin to become aware of just how much you encounter it in your day-to-day life.

You deal with projection from experts on TV telling you how to run your love life, your friend telling you what to eat, the person in the grocery store line telling you what we should be doing in Israel, a newspaper article telling you how to sleep in the proper manner, a physical therapist telling you how to walk the right way, your parents telling you what job you should get, and a cacophony of subconscious beliefs being projected onto you in a never-ending stream.

Is it any wonder that we have become rather robotic in our approach to life and living? The average person believes and lives by all of the projections that she is bombarded with every single day of her life. And, when someone believes the projections she is being programmed with, she will, in turn, project them onto you.

The first step to transcending projection is to realize how many times a day you, yourself, are telling other people how to live their lives. The second step is to learn the adage, "The best advice given is advice asked for." The meaning of this is that people will only ever truly listen to your advice when they have asked for it first. Otherwise, it's like spraying water against a concrete wall, hoping that the water will get to the garden on the other side of it. Thus, waiting for someone to ask for your advice first is like removing the concrete wall in front of the garden. Then and only then will someone actually listen to you.

The third step in this process is learning how to "share" instead of "tell." When you share your advice, you are sharing your personal truth about an issue, as opposed to trying to make your truth into their truth. Instead of "You need to" or "You should" you can replace it with "This is what worked for me" or "Well, if it were me, I would…" You will get their attention and their respect and perhaps even add value to their life when you share information in this way.

Becoming aware of projecting is an important step in your conscious evolution because it helps you to create a safe space where people will feel free to drop their guards with you and engage in authentic communication. This means that instead of telling you what they think they should or what they think you want to hear, they will tell you how they honestly feel about something. This is worth its weight in gold due to the fact that you can only move forward in any type of relationship through the medium of emotional honesty and authenticity.

Otherwise, you are simply engaged in role-play with each other and bouncing surface level projections back and forth. This form of quiet insanity has pervaded human consciousness for long enough, and the time for emotionally honest communication is at hand.

8

Unconscious Reactivity

A primary impetus for the argument of elevating your consciousness is to absolve what Zen Master Vernon Kitabu Turner alluded to as "push-button consciousness" in his book *Soul Sword: Way and Mind of a Zen Warrior.* In this state of consciousness, you are essentially a walking "button" waiting to be pushed by external stimuli.

All anybody needs to do is push one of your emotional buttons to elicit an immediate response. In this state of consciousness, you are so deeply unconscious that you are helpless to your emotional triggers. Any person can accidentally push one of your buttons at any time and you will simply react. Your life is on autopilot, and you are a virtual sleepwalker. Another description of this level of consciousness would be "complete helplessness." You have no control over your life and are at the mercy of your unhealed emotional body.

As an example, if you are a male who happens to suffer from insecurity and/or fears confrontation, when another male accidentally bumps into you on the sidewalk, you will most likely unconsciously react. You react immediately due to the fact that you have an unhealed suppressed emotional charge (or many) around your inability to stand up for yourself or your need to prove yourself. You take it personally as if it's an affront to your worthiness to exist. You may become very angry or even physically assault the person if the emotional wound is strong enough. Or, if your fear of confrontation is strong enough, you may simply give him or her a dirty look while, underneath, you are both fearful of the confrontation and simultaneously angry with yourself for feeling the fear. Either way, it is fear-based in that you are defending against either your fear that you are not worthy or your fear of confrontation.

Another example could be if you are a mother who is trying desperately to multi-task your job and your children. If you are deeply unconscious, when your child wants your attention at the end of a long day, you may instantly react with anger. In this case your internal dialogue is "Why can't people just give me a break?" or you may project onto your child the thought "You are ungrateful!"

Either way, it is an unconscious reaction that results in the transference of emotional patterning to children who will then grow up to replicate this same cycle with their own children. It's nobody's "fault" per se; it's simply the result of a level of consciousness that means emotional pain is a regular way of life. In this instance, the mother's life will continue on in this manner until some form of inner catalyst or strong enough desire for a different way of life occurs.

What she does not know is that the simple act of taking five minutes to be fully present with the children when she gets home would absolve the entire issue. Taking five minutes for herself in the morning upon waking and before she gets the children up, to just "be" will result in a completely alternate life path. You may be tempted to think

"That's easy for you to say," and yet I assure you this is the truth. Taking the time to just "be" is a powerful method of diffusing unconscious reactivity. Convincing someone to do this is much more difficult, though.

Of course, the more deeply unconscious the person is, the less likely it will be that the catalyst will be consciously sought after. In other words, if you are deeply unconscious, then your catalyst will probably be a result of an extremely emotionally painful experience that occurs unexpectedly. It often takes many years after the fact to realize what a "blessing" this experience was in your life. You can reflect, looking backwards, at how your life-path took a completely different direction starting from that fateful day when the powerful catalyst for awakening was presented to you.

The Catalyst

For me it was the strong identification with my physical body as my persona that led to the catalyst for my transformation. The physical result was that I tore my shoulder and could no longer build and develop my body. It created a great rift inside of me that I was forced to enter into in search of the meaning for my existence. It lasted a full decade, whereupon in the meantime, I tried every single modality known to man to heal my wounded shoulder, but to no avail. Nothing worked, not even surgery. It was finally decided that this injury must be karmic in nature and that I needed to transcend it rather than continue trying to heal it.

Along the way, I was forced to completely redefine who I was and what my mission in life was. It was my own personal catalyst for transformation into a more powerful Being with much more to offer the world. It forced me to face myself at the deepest possible level. I came face to face with the bottomless abyss that is fear. The illusion is that, when you are looking into it, it appears bottomless. The reality is that just on the other side of fear is freedom. Just on the other side of the darkness is the light. This is what was meant by the adage "Behind our greatest fears lie our greatest rewards." Moving through your fear could be the most amazing thing that you ever do for yourself. It is also the quickest and most direct route to becoming conscious and awakened.

Understandably, many people say that going on a "Fire Walk" with Tony Robbins is an incredibly transformational and life-altering experience. Doing this puts you in a forced confrontation with fear. Any time you can do this, it translates into the catalyst for a powerful expansion of mind that has an amazingly positive impact upon your life. However, this type of experience is one that must be consciously sought after. If your level of consciousness is not evolved enough to the point where you are purposefully seeking to confront your inner fears, then you will not likely go to an event like this. The less developed levels of consciousness are usually personified by the act of day-to-day survival.

Stimulus/Response

The lowest level of consciousness, where you are deeply unconsciously reactive, is like "hell on earth." There is quite simply no more painful way to exist than by way of "stimulus/response." In this mode of living, you are learning solely by the stimulus of pain or pleasure. You move towards pleasure and away from pain. In this base level of consciousness, you are more susceptible to addictive behaviors due to the fact that they appear to simultaneously help you elude pain and

AUTHENTIC POWER THROUGH SPIRITUALITY

gain pleasure. Since everything seems to appear to come from outside of you at this level of awareness, then the experience of feeling "helpless" often accompanies it. Most people at this level have nowhere near the ability to take responsibility for the reality that they are creating, so they turn to addictive behaviors to diminish the feeling of pain. Life for most at this level is a vicious cycle of desperately seeking pleasure while running away from pain.

The way out for most is by hitting "rock bottom" where they awaken to the fact that they "cannot keep on like this." It's like the heroin addict who wakes up literally in the gutter. This time the magnitude of the negative experience proves to be a strong enough catalyst to desire transformation. The experience was painful enough that it creates a temporary window into present moment awareness, which becomes the gateway to a better way of life.

Unless this catalyst occurs, most individuals at this level of consciousness will continue on within their vicious cycles. As an outsider who perhaps has had enough life experience to embody a relatively higher level of consciousness, you may be wondering how you can be of aid to people in these situations. If your consciousness has not sufficiently evolved to the point where you can effect powerful change for a neighborhood or community with your presence, you may dive in unaware of the potential pitfalls to exposing yourself to this type of energy.

What many people do with the best of intentions is to succumb to their own subconscious inner "should" dialogue. There may actually be an intention to help or be of service on the surface, but it is often an unhealed emotional projection coming from within their unaddressed emotional issues. In essence, this person wants to save the community because he or she believes that they should, not because they are passionate about it. So, instead of continuing to evolve their own consciousness and getting to a point where they can create some real change in the community, they wade into the unconscious energy in attempts to save the world. The problem is that they very quickly become overwhelmed when they realize that there is a streaming mass of unhealed people who are eager to take what you have to give. In turn, this begins to create the feeling of anger and bitterness toward the world for not being more compassionate by "wading in with them and lending a hand." They begin thinking in terms of "I am down here helping and sacrificing my own life, so why aren't you doing it too?" In the meantime, they completely miss the fact that they are not at the level of consciousness where they can effect permanent change for their community. If anything, at this level of consciousness, they are often enacting a codependency instead.

This means that people will simply come to rely upon them for aid in whatever form they are providing it. The deeply unconscious hordes will come and take what you have in attempts to fill their own emotional voids, without the slightest thought to your well-being or any attempt to evolve themselves in any way. It is not a judgment; it is simply a level of consciousness. Thus, to effect real change, one must evolve oneself first, the world second.

As people begin to evolve themselves and become aware of how many times a day they unconsciously enact some form of subconscious behavior or react to some form of emotional stimuli, then they become part of the solution instead of the problem. As you bring your unconscious to light, you also bring more potential healing and solutions to light for the people around you whom you interact with. This is yet another way in which you can begin to build authentic power as well as become the change you want to see in the world.

9

Karma

Another confusing and convoluted topic is "karma." For many people, the word karma means something along the lines of "you reap what you sow." Most people believe that karma is the reaction to something you did that was "bad." So, if you do something bad to someone, then, in turn, something bad will happen to you. This belief is so pervasive that many people believe they are suffering from the karma of past life events and even use this premise as a way to disown their power to change events within their current ones.

Some people will even go so far as to tell you when they think the reason a negative event has recently occurred within *your* life is due to a karmic repercussion. "Sounds like bad karma" is the response you may elicit from a friend when you inform them you were rear-ended at the light yesterday. The result is people often believe that, in order for you to be going through the challenging events in your life, which you are, you must have done *something* to deserve it.

Another typical mass mind response is "What did you do?" when confiding in a friend about a situation where someone reacted in a negative way toward you. The unconscious assumption is that you must have, again, done *something* to get the other person to say or react the way they did toward you.

It's true that we are the creators of our own life experience, but saying that we deserve what we get is a little out of context. It creates the idea of "punishment" which is not at all what karma is. Rather, karma is the residual energy around you that has been built up over your lifetime (perhaps lifetimes), which pulls in events and life situations that are a vibrational match.

In other words, if you have done things that have created positive impacts within other people's lives, the results of doing this have created good feelings for you. In turn, these accumulated feelings have built up a positive energy around you that is charged and magnetic. This means that it is actively now pulling in people, places, and things that are also positive.

Additionally, you can feel it around you. Conversely, if you have done things that have created negative impacts within other people's lives, this energy will build up within you over time according to how many people you have affected and how deeply you affected them. In the same way that the positive energy is charged and magnetic, so is the negative energy. Thus, you could also create some negative, karmic energy around you that is magnetic to situations that are not pleasing. There is no judgment of "good" or "bad;" it is simply residual energy which is magnetic to like energy and which you have created over a period of time.

The way out is not to disown your power, but to move through it with grace by utilizing awareness and mind/ body sciences. Thus, instead of relegating yourself to being a victim of circumstance by seeking to understand why this is happening to you, you confront the life lessons head on by taking empowering action-steps. Understanding why you may be suffering from some sort of karmic event is only constructive if it leads you to taking a course of action. Otherwise, you run the risk of entrenching yourself within the ideal of negative karma through the self-victimization of believing that you deserve what you are getting. Often times what accompanies this state of mind is the self-validation of not taking any actions to change your circumstances.

If you can rationalize that you are deserving of negative karma, then you can further rationalize not taking any actions to change your circumstances. Now the individual is free to play the role of "martyr" without having to worry about ever confronting his/her life lessons. This is an unfortunate byproduct of the misunderstanding or, perhaps, *misuse* of the term "karma."

Good Things Happen to Bad People!

Now, that said, it's also true that karma does play a role in the shaping of our lives and destinies. It is possible that you or someone you know is dealing with some karmic repercussions from events in this lifetime or even a past lifetime. For instance, some people argue that bad things happen to good people while simultaneously good things happen to bad people. The problem is that we never see the entire picture of anyone's life or *lifetimes*. We have no idea what this person did or did not do in their past ten lifetimes incarnating upon the Earth or, for that matter, what their life looked like before we met them in this one.

You do not know if the really good person you are referring to, who seems to be suffering through some seemingly unfair events, was actually a mass murderer in his past lifetime. It may be challenging to think in these terms or even a little "woo-woo" for some people, and yet there is good documentation for the premise of reincarnation. If you read anything by Dr. Michael Newton or Brian Weiss, M.D., it may sufficiently expand your consciousness to the point where you begin to question some of the subconscious beliefs that were given to you as a child before you had the power of choice.

If you think about it, lots of unbelievable things have occurred in the past one thousand years. For instance, we discovered the world is round, not flat; we discovered that the sun revolves around the earth, not the other way around; we broke the four minute mile when we believed it could never be done; we created air travel when we believed it was not possible; we split the atom when most scientists could not even conceive of it; we broke the speed of sound when we didn't think human beings could ever go that fast; we put men on the moon when we would have laughed at you for even suggesting the idea, and we elected a black president when no one thought it could ever happen.

Really, the list is endless, but prior to accomplishing or discovering these things, we had the belief that it could not be done or that it was not true. In my opinion, it's not about "beliefs," it's about expanding your consciousness. This means that, ultimately, you must transcend all beliefs in order to fully actualize yourself.

Reincarnation

For me, the level of consciousness that becomes aware of, questions, rejects, and finally accepts reincarnation as a fact of life, was achieved and subsequently moved beyond a long time ago. For some people, the idea is liberating and for others, it is challenging. The reason that it's liberating is that it may offer some a relief from the pressure of feeling as if they need to get everything exactly right in this lifetime. In other words, it may provide the ability to relax and enjoy the journey of life a bit more. For others, the idea is challenging because it is contrary to what they were taught or programmed to believe as children.

Most of our beliefs were given to us before we had the opportunity to choose them. This means that, when you are defending an ideal or a belief, you may not even be defending something that you consciously agree with. You may only be defending a program installed into your subconscious by someone else. Were you given the conscious opportunity to identify and examine each one of your beliefs with nonattachment, perhaps you might agree with some of them.

However, my contingency is that, if you had been given the conscious choice, you might not have agreed with any of the beliefs you were given as a child, all of which are operating subconsciously today. Yet, my job is not to rearrange your beliefs, but to help you to expand your consciousness. If this concept is too challenging for you, then you are free to skip it for now since everything you need in order to change is happening right now regardless.

Born Knowing

If you've ever witnessed or known people who are born with extraordinary abilities or with wisdom that seems beyond their years, then you have been given a glimpse into reincarnation. It's simply because some folks have been around for a long, long time and have had the opportunity to refine a skill or evolve their consciousness throughout many lifetimes. This is often the case of the "child prodigy" or the individual who knows from age three what she wants to do for the entire rest of her life. These people are born remembering what they are passionate about due to the fact that they have been focused upon it for lifetime after lifetime, refining their skill and coming to mastery within their craft. When this is the case, there are usually three clues that come together which represent this type of Soul: first, they are very adept at doing what they set out to do. Second, they seem to be solely focused upon mastering one single craft. Third, they demonstrate a higher level of awareness beginning from the time that they are able to speak.

Alternately, some Souls have been incarnating for a long time because of their *lack* of ability to grasp or master a certain concept or skill. In this case, a Soul may be attempting to master a craft, learn a lesson, or confront a certain type of situation that continues to pop up in their life. An example could be a person who is trying to master the lesson of jealousy. They are deeply insecure about themselves and also about feeling vulnerable in relationships. So, lifetime after lifetime, they attract to themselves, partners who challenge this insecurity with their propensity to flirt and/ or to be emotionally independent.

In this way, they attract the type of person who both most deeply triggers this issue within them and also provides for them the chance to confront it. However, instead of allowing themselves to be with their fear and insecurity, they lash out at their partner in attempts to gain control. This could be verbal confrontation, psychological manipulation, verbal abuse, physical intimidation, or even physical abuse. When this happens, they fail the lesson. And, if their partner continues to tolerate it indefinitely, then they will carry this lesson into the next lifetime. This could continue on for many lifetimes until a big enough trigger is presented and the lesson can no longer go ignored. The entire process is about evolving your consciousness and working through life lessons to the point where you don't need to anymore.

I've met those rare individuals who appear to be closing in on their last few incarnations and, who by simply being in close physical proximity seem to make you feel more at peace. Of course, I've spent enough time around many brand new Souls who often border on obnoxious due to a combination of the excitement of incarnating mixed with a base level of consciousness. There is nothing wrong with any level of consciousness, as all phases are valid and simply a part of the journey.

As an example, the homeless guy on the corner could be a high level Soul who is working on mastering the lesson of "nonattachment," or he could be a brand new Soul who cannot cope with physical reality. Either is possible, but usually a key indicator is how much peaceful or creative energy is or is not radiating from the individual.

There is still quite a bit which is unknown when it comes to reincarnation since it is very rare to experience your past lives in your current one. For instance, we usually do not know how many incarnations we've had, when we started as a Soul, or when we're going to complete our life lessons and ascend into the next dimension of existence. It is possible to get a general idea of your own progress by looking at how many difficulties you have had in your current life and how successfully you have or have not been able to navigate them. Some higher-level souls are given more to work through in a given incarnation because they are able to successfully navigate the life lessons and challenges. Other, newer Souls, who have not been incarnating as much, have difficulty with the bare minimum of obtaining a job and taking care of themselves. As per normal, I am making gross overgeneralizations, as the possible combinations of different types of life lessons are virtually endless. It's always possible a higher-level Soul could get snagged up on a basic lesson and, as a result, have spent two dozen incarnations attempting to work through it.

One way to gauge if you have been putting off a particular life lesson for a long time is by getting in touch with how great the fear is of confronting and working through that issue. If the fear is great, there could be a chance that you have been trying to confront this issue for many lifetimes, and it is a lingering issue. This could also mean that working through this issue will be extremely rewarding and provide you with an amazing sense of freedom and expansion of your consciousness.

Although potentially challenging, and mostly due to mass mind programming that we received as children, embracing the concept of reincarnation can and will begin to unlock more of your latent talents and abilities. This is so is because the mere act of opening yourself to this concept will allow you to open previously locked doors within your mind. Most people are nowhere near bringing their full power to bear when it comes to achieving goals and living a full life. By opening to the idea that we are multidimensional beings who have been incarnating for a long time, we open the doors to becoming much more than we ever possibly imagined.

10

Manifestation

Initially, I began studying spirituality because I thought that it would help me to achieve my dreams and goals. I struggled to try to make something out of my life while I continued running face first into my own subconscious sabotage mechanisms. I knew there was something missing from the equation, but I just couldn't seem to put my finger on what that thing was. So when someone introduced me to my first self-help book *The Achievement Zone* by Dr. Shane Murphy, I was instantly hooked. It was eye opening to me to discover there were authors writing about the exact things that I seemed to have problems with. I felt as if I had stumbled onto a secret pathway that would surely lead to everything that I had ever dreamed of.

I then found *The Road Less Traveled* by M. Scott Peck, which was even more profound, and life altering for me. In turn, this eventually led me to *The Power of Your Subconscious Mind* by Dr. Joseph Murphy. This book was the most intriguing of all to me because it was written by a Spiritual Minister whose core message seemed to be, "You should be able to have whatever you want in your life." This was a profound statement since my previous understanding was that you could not be a spiritual person and simultaneously allow yourself to have or desire more money than you needed to survive. In one fell swoop, my belief system around money was completely shifted. More importantly, this book became the gateway into spirituality for me by bridging the gap between the material and spiritual worlds. I did not set out to understand spirituality, but instead stumbled upon it while I was trying to figure out how to become successful.

In the beginning, all I wanted to understand was how to get my life together, make more money, and achieve my goals. I had zero interest in spirituality, mind/body science, or learning about being "guided" by my "intuition." I considered these subjects to be too "woo woo" and never took them seriously. In fact, for the most part I didn't want to hear anything even remotely spirituality related.

I'm not certain about the origin of this resistance, but it likely had something to do with my anti-establishment upbringing. In turn, this led to an "anti-spiritual" approach to life. Ironically, my parents' dislike of established religion became indirectly associated with spirituality and created a negative connotation for me with the topic. This is most likely why I had to be "tricked" into reading about spirituality because if you had told me that I was reading a "spiritual book" I would have probably put it down.

It took some time to realize, upon hindsight looking back, that many of the spiritual writers I had been following had disguised themselves as "self-help" writers. These authors were clearly aware of what motivated people and leveraged this as a way to open people's minds to something greater. In some ways you could even consider it as manipulative, but I only felt gratitude for the fact that I was able to follow the path laid out before me and read some of these amazing works.

The Law of Attraction

Somewhere along the way, I started to encounter metaphysical philosophies like "the law of attraction" and "manifestation." I became enamored with the potential to use your mind to create your reality and manifest things into existence. Specifically, I studied the law of attraction philosophy in depth and spent many hours reading various books and teachings on the subject. I began to implement the philosophy and related techniques in my life on a regular basis. I found the philosophy to be empowering, but the results to be intangible and ephemeral. It appeared to me that sometimes things did seem to happen according to the teachings. Other times, it seemed as if nothing happened at all.

Then, there were also teachings that seemed to rationalize the times when things did not appear to happen. If things happened the way you wanted them to, then you were correctly utilizing the law of attraction. However, if things did not happen the way you wanted them to, then you were incorrectly using it. So there was certain "convenience" to the philosophy in that you could never definitively prove one way or the other if it was actually working. It did appear to me, however, that the more an individual believed he or she was going to manifest a thing, the more likelihood it would happen.

This meant that the law of attraction definitely worked better for those people who had an easier time believing that good things would happen in their lives. But this begged the question: *What about the people who needed the most help, the ones whose lives had never really been going well, and as result, had a more difficult time believing that they ever would?*

As a result of this, I began to feel as if there might be a problem with the way the *philosophy* of the law of attraction was being presented in that it seemed to invite some people to make a spiritual bypass. As an example, desperate individuals could become attached to the idea of manifesting, to the point where they were engaging less and less with their physical lives. In turn, instead of confronting the impending issues within their physical lives by taking the necessary action-steps, they would engage the law of attraction philosophy.

Or, on the other hand, if it were an individual who needed to confront emotional issues that were crippling her ability to confront reality, she might become attached to the seemingly simple solution, which the law of attraction appeared to provide. This would result in the avoidance of the confrontation of emotional pain by, again, making the spiritual bypass.

When this happened to people who had not done the necessary inner work on their emotional bodies, it could create a roller coaster of emotional highs and lows. This transpired because the individual was trying in vain to "manifest" their reality by forcing themselves to feel positive emotions, which they were not authentically feeling. Or, they were trying to consciously believe something that they did not subconsciously believe was possible.

However, I also recognized great value in the philosophy of the law of attraction because it got people thinking outside the box, helped them to feel more deserving and worthy, and turned them onto the spiritual path. The law of attraction is a real phenomenon in that, on a quantum level, we are vibrational magnets, drawing experiences to ourselves. These experiences are a vibrational match to all of the mental and emotional energy we are holding onto and projecting outwards. The catch is that the vast majority of this energy is subconscious. This means that when you start trying to project positive energy and emotions onto life situations that you desire to change, it's possible for you to get into a pitched battle with your subconscious mind, which runs at least 90% of the show. It can be incredibly frustrating to try your heart out with visualizing positive outcomes, projecting positive energy, and putting on the happy face, only to find in the end that nothing has changed in your life.

In an extreme example, if someone who suffers from deep depression discovers the law of attraction, it can have a very adverse effect. This is because the deeper levels of depression often come from deeply unhealed emotional issues or unresolved life situations that need to be consciously addressed. When a person with this condition or life situations attempts to use the law of attraction philosophy in order to feel better, it's possible to have it backfire on them and leave them feeling emotionally debilitated. This is because, prior to this event, they were likely in a space of relative acceptance of the feeling of deep depression and their battle with depression. However, moving from that space, to the space of allowing oneself to feel hope; only to slide back into the anguish of deep depression, is almost more than most people can bear.

Whatever the situation may be, it is always more damaging to those people who have felt helpless for a long time, to finally feel some hope in their lives, only to land back in the same situation they were at in the beginning.

This is, perhaps, the biggest potential repercussion for those people who attempt to use the law of attraction philosophy as a spiritual bypass mechanism. When someone allows herself to feel hope for the first time in a long time about changing the circumstances in her life, and then winds up right back where she started, not only does she feel worse, but now the belief that she is helpless to change her life is often stronger. The potential repercussion is someone who feels more pessimistic, depressed, and disempowered than previously.

The Integrated Law of Attraction

Some people will have no trouble whatsoever utilizing the law of attraction and manifesting desired outcomes in their lives. In fact, for many people, the law of attraction has come along as a pleasant reminder of something they felt they already 'knew' at a deeper level. For these people the idea of manifestation and law of attraction brings the freedom of expression and creation. Ultimately this is the goal for all people in the world, to be able to create and manifest their hearts desires. So for these ones who are able to simply pick up this powerful tool and begin utilizing it at will to manifest their lives the way they want it, no change is needed. They may have already done the necessary clearing work and not have as many subconscious beliefs and/or unhealed emotions within their subconscious. This means they are free to create at will.

However, for the people who have had trouble with it, I suggest a more integrated approach when applying its principles. The very first thing I suggest is to make a game out of it. Do not use it to save your life, but instead use it to see if you can begin to make some small changes. You do this by using it just to see what happens, without being overly attached to any outcomes.

The next thing I suggest is not to use it as a means to feel better if you have unhealed emotional issues or repressed emotions from childhood. When you do this, you are trying to force positive emotions onto an un-evolved emotional body. Instead, utilize something like my emotional integration technique to heal suppressed emotional charges and integrate fragmented aspects of your psyche. If you have deeply unhealed issues and begin utilizing the law of attraction, these issues will surface very quickly to let you know that you are not ready to move into an abundance mind frame just yet. Otherwise, these heavy, unhealed emotional issues will simply pull you back down.

When people try this and find themselves falling into emotional pitfalls, it's like they are trying to set sail with the anchor still down. In other words, you won't get anywhere or make any progress under these circumstances. You must release and integrate any deeply unhealed issues within your emotional body, or you will inevitably come crashing back down. The integrated approach to the law of attraction is using it as a playful means to see what you can do while, in the meantime, you also work on healing and evolving your emotional body. In this way, you will get the double benefits of healing your emotional body and returning your life to being a fun game simultaneously.

Life was meant to be fun and the law of attraction, when used playfully and lightheartedly, can help to return some of the joy to the game of life. If things have been emotionally heavy for you and you've had to deal with anxiety, depression, frustration, or grief, then you may wish to take time to heal and integrate your emotional body. This way you will not risk bypassing any unhealed emotions and allow yourself to experience the healing that you deserve.

11

The Emotional Body

Perhaps the most significant and, yet most misunderstood element of human consciousness is the *emotional body*. In our modern day society, we are encouraged and praised for our over-mentalization of the simplest things. This means that we have become driven to *think* that we can think our way out of, or into any situation. Instead of gently feeling our way through life via our natural intuitive capacity, we are encouraged to aggressively think our way through it. When the mind begins to dominate, we become more neurotic and obsessive in our thinking and actions. This means that we no longer allow solutions to come to us, but instead force an outcome through mentalization. The problem is that when we *force* an outcome or a solution, it will always only be temporary.

The mind cannot, of itself, come up with a solution. It can only process data that has already been uploaded into it. Thus, when we become over-mentalized or overly identified with our thinking, we seal ourselves off from higher levels of our own innate intelligence. Another way of saying this is that the same level of thinking that created the problem will not be able to solve it. When, instead, the mind is used as a receiver and processor for higher levels of intelligence, it is fulfilling its role perfectly.

The phrase "clear your mind" really means, "clear your mind so that you can receive higher intelligence and real solutions."

The real question though is *what are you trying to clear your mind from?* The answer is "thoughts." When you try to clear your mind, ironically, you are trying to clear it of thoughts. Yet, we are taught to use our mind to think our way through life. *So, which is it?* Are thoughts good? Or, are they bad? It's interesting to think about thinking. The answer is that thoughts are neither good nor bad. They simply "are." It is our mind that has become addicted to thinking.

When this occurs we begin to feel more isolated, neurotic, and compulsive in how we live our lives. Our life starts to become a cycle at first, then later, a vicious cycle. The very definition of "hell on earth" is living the same life over and over again as a result of thinking the same thoughts over and over again, without a way to change it.

An even better question is, "What is controlling my mind?" The answer is surprising: the emotional body. The emotional body is who's really running the show. However, it would be more correct to say that the unhealed emotional body is running the show. You could even take it to a slightly deeper level by saying that our suppressed emotional charges and emotional patterning from childhood are running the show. Either way, it's all conveniently located and stored within your emotional body.

Access Key

Since we are asking a lot of questions in this chapter, perhaps the best question of all is; how do I heal and evolve my emotional body? For most people this can seem very daunting and perhaps even potentially arduous since we have been trained to completely ignore the emotional body. Developing the ability to "feel" is paramount to your personal evolution and expansion of consciousness. Without exercising this muscle, you will simply not be able to move forward. This is because, the more unhealed your emotional body is, the more deeply suppressed your emotional charges are. This means that they will stay within you, unconsciously, and continue to create unpleasing circumstances for you throughout your life without you understanding why it is happening. Without allowing these suppressed emotional charges to surface for integration, they will remain in your bio-energetic field where they will magnetize other people with similar issues to you.

In extreme cases, traumatic emotional events are repressed and pushed more deeply into the subconscious mind, where they become completely unconscious. This means there is a deep dissociation from the event or emotional injury to the point where the person is completely dis-identified with it. In turn, this means that this person will, for a good portion of her life, live unconsciously and not comprehend why things happen the way they do and simultaneously feel like a victim of outside circumstances.

The examples are as varied as they are endless. To illustrate the point, we will use a classic example of a woman who was molested as a child. As she gets older, the fragmented aspect of her psyche that was created when this event happened, which has become a "sub-personality," becomes more active. Its job is to protect her from ever having anything remotely like this event ever happen to her again in life. It discovers that, if she has a larger, less attractive physical body, that she does not get as much attention from potential threats. Thus, it begins to feed her thoughts, whatever thoughts work to get the job done, which will trigger her to unconsciously engage in activities that will make her put weight onto her body.

And so, by the time she is eighteen years old, she has become overweight and is considered physically unattractive by societal standards. Subconsciously, she is right on track to keep herself safe; however, this agenda contradicts her conscious desire to feel physically attractive and have a partner. So begins the war with herself, where she tries every diet imaginable and every exercise program conceivable, only to wind up right back where she started. This continues on and on, occasionally feeling as if she is finally "on the right track" only to, yet again, wind up back where she started.

The problem is that she is not addressing the real reason why she is overweight. The real reason is that there is a part of her which does not feel "safe" feeling attractive. Since sub-personalities are subconscious, she is not consciously aware that it exists. She is completely unaware that the real reason she cannot lose any weight is because she is in a pitched battle with a part of herself.

She does not understand why, in sudden moments of awareness that come and go, she becomes aware of the compulsion to eat when she is not hungry. During these rare moments, she asks herself, *"Why did I do that?"* She doesn't understand why she suddenly feels tired at the mere thought of exercising. It is not because she is lazy, rather it's because there is an unhealed, fragmented aspect of her psyche that needs integration. If this integration never happens, she will never be able to lose the weight. Even surgery, if she decides to go a more drastic direction, will only prove a temporary solution.

Another example could be the adult man who is fearful of confrontation. As a child, he was yelled at by his father to the point of tears, or perhaps even physically abused repeatedly. This is an example of subconscious "emotional patterning" where the child is repeatedly imprinted with the event over a period of time. As he grows up, he realizes that he is internally fearful of confrontation but remains unable to make the connection as to why this is so. He does not understand that he has been imprinted with an emotional pattern that engages upon being encountered with a certain set of stimuli.

To complicate matters, he feels fine most of the time, which means that, when the stimulus is encountered, it feels as if this powerful fear of confrontation comes out of nowhere. However, any time he gets into a situation where he is forced to confront someone or he is verbally yelled at, his childhood programming is triggered, and he is reduced to the little boy who was verbally intimidated by his father. In this way, he suddenly becomes overwhelmed with fear and completely helpless to the subconscious programming he received as a child.

The tricky thing about emotional imprinting vs. suppressed emotional charges is that it is often more problematic to integrate. Sometimes, it will require a combination of a mind/body science practice mixed with physical action-steps to move through it symbolically in order for total integration to occur. This means that if someone wants to heal, he must be willing to think in terms of the journey and not the destination. Emotional imprinting, when speaking from the most deeply entrenched potential, must be engaged as a "work in progress." It could take an entire lifetime to release the patterning that causes you to unconsciously react to the emotional trigger. However, as you engage with this journey, you will experience relative degrees of emotional freedom as you begin to unfold the layers of patterning at deeper levels within your subconscious.

The Business of Emotion

In society, men are taught to be tough and not to show emotion. To do so is to be considered a "lesser man" in the eyes of your male counterparts. Of course, on a business scale, this plays into corporate greed and a total dissociation from the repercussions of creating massive global companies that negatively impact the environment and enslave entire populations of indigenous peoples. Disassociation with the emotional body creates the need for war and domination because, when people cannot "feel" anything, they will do anything. If you do not have the capacity to "feel," then you do not feel the pain that you create.

The reality is that, for these corporate monsters, they do feel the pain that they create; they are merely unconscious of it. This means that they are creating pain for themselves and others, but are internally blocked from the conscious experience of this pain. However, this pain builds within them and ultimately manifests as some form of massive adversity through either illness or another problem. It can literally become a cancer inside of you that is eating away at your body.

In order to compete in the market place, many women have opted to attempt to close themselves off from their ability to "feel" as well. When this happens, the result is a woman who is embracing the masculine aspect of herself but at the total expense of her natural feminine ability to feel. These women often become hardened and dissociated from the repercussions of their actions, much as their male counterparts. They are more likely to do whatever it takes to climb the corporate ladder in order to gain power, favor, and all in the name of external validation. At a deeper level unconsciously, this is actually the attempt to gain approval from their male counterparts, which, in turn, is driven by the societal subconscious belief that men are somehow more deserving and worthy.

When viewed holistically, one begins to see part of the mechanism through which war, famine, and greed have gained a historic foothold in the world. When we allow ourselves to subconsciously believe that "thinking" is superior to "feeling," and we associate thinking with "male" and "feeling" with female, then we can see how our infatuation with thinking has led to our demise. In a completely unconscious way, it supports our subconscious belief that men are superior to women in the business place. In turn, this validates both men and women to take on a more masculine and, as a result, more emotionally closed-off role in business.

This means that our business model has historically been more ego-driven and less intuitively developed. The results speak for themselves: mindless consumerism, corporate corruption, mass pollution, and vast populations of people in poverty. The only thing that needs to occur in order to reverse the entire process is the added element of "feminine" energy into the business world. When this happens, the world will change in more profound ways than most people can possibly fathom.

12

Feminine and Masculine Energy

In Taoism the balance between the feminine and masculine energy is described as the "yin and yang." The symbol is drawn in such a way as to represent how they both play an equal and intertwined role within a person's life. In our westernized lifestyle, the masculine energy, through over-mentalization, has taken a larger role than is healthy. This is represented by the compulsive identification with our thoughts as "who we are."

As previously described, this leads to the disassociation from the repercussions of our actions. It also means that we think in much smaller circles and utilize a much smaller percentage of our innately higher levels of intelligence. Another way to describe it would be like saying that the waves on the surface of the ocean represent the masculine energy, while the depths of the ocean represent the feminine energy. When we repress our feminine side, we close ourselves off to the depths of our consciousness. We limit ourselves to the small, endless waves on the surface, crashing into each other, in a ceaseless, chaotic stream of unending thoughts.

The masculine side need not be demonized, however. Both sides play an important role and, when properly balanced, will nurture you in positive ways. For instance, embracing your masculine side can help you to create healthy boundaries by learning that it is okay to say "no" to people. It can also help you to physically defend yourself or to build a business. Embracing your masculine side can empower you to become an entrepreneur, to get out there and go for it. In other words, the masculine side is needed in order to have the motivation to take the physical action steps it requires to build something.

Embracing your feminine side can help you to get more in touch with your emotional body. Or, on a more practical level, it can help you to have a better relationship with your wife. It can help you to appreciate nature. Your masculine side could drive you to become an entrepreneur, but your feminine side could provide for you the idea that helps millions of people's lives become easier and result in millions of dollars in your checking account.

The masculine side could not have thought of this because it comes from beyond ordinary thought. Conversely, the feminine side is where all creativity and beauty comes from. All art and poetry comes from the feminine side exclusively. Also, the ability to appreciate these things comes from the feminine side as well.

Thus, when you look at the picture holistically, you see the value of having a good balance between the two energies. A more simplified way of looking at it could be this: the more balanced the person, the more successful he will be. Of course, this is a drastic oversimplification of viewing this balance because there are endless definitions of what we refer to as "success." In general, though, success in this regard means a fulfilling life in your relationships, creativity, finance, and career. In other words, striking the balance between the masculine and feminine parts of yourself usually means that you are more prone to nurture every facet of your life equally.

ALIVE AWAKE AWARE

13

Relationships

When it comes to creating your reality and building your life the way you want it to be, an integral piece of this puzzle is almost always your personal relationship, or relationships. Most people are taught to believe that we are supposed to find one single person and make him or her into our partner for the entire rest of our lives.

The reality, of course, is that life is not so simple, nor was it meant to be. The thing about all of the subconscious beliefs that have been programmed into us at a societal level is that, at the next phase of growth and development, they cease to continue working. Thus, what has served to make us into a better, more efficient species one day becomes a limitation.

The belief that we are meant to be with one special person for our entire lifetime is an example of this. This belief helped us to bring order out of the chaos for many hundreds of years. From this one, basic subconscious belief, we were able to create entire nations, develop cultures, and create societies. However, it was always based upon a subconscious belief: *you need to find the man or woman who is right for you and get married, immediately.* Historically, this was usually followed by: *And have at least two children to carry on your legacy.*

For many people this belief still works just fine. In fact, there is nothing inherently wrong with this belief. It's only when it forces you to do something that, in your heart, you do not really want to do that it begins to create dysfunction. In other words, when your subconscious belief forces you into a relationship or marriage while in your heart your desire is to experience the freedom of solitude, it begins to restrict your potential growth and expansion. It's not to say that freedom cannot be experienced within a committed relationship. Rather, it's to say that there is a certain type of freedom that is only to be found in the solitude of total self-reliance in every way that this means.

For some people, this is an authentic desire that comes from a soul-level need. This means that the desire is authentic and valid and that to deny this desire is to create emotional pain for themselves. Another way of looking at this is to say that, when it's time for you to begin to transcend your subconscious beliefs and you do not allow yourself to out of fear, you will begin to feel the emotional pain of constriction. That pain is the small or "ego-identified self" usurping the needs of the large "Self," or "soul-identified self."

Alone Time

Many people, during this time period of massively shifting consciousness, transition, and vibrational acceleration, are awakening to the need for more time spent alone in reflection, meditation, and self-nurturing. To reiterate this means, however, that they will come face to face with the subconscious belief that they are *supposed* to be in a relationship. Often, this internal battle is projected outwards onto the people around them. What this means is they will begin to recruit people to role-play with them, externally, the beliefs which they are holding onto internally. If their consciousness is not yet evolved to the point where they can internalize this debate and ultimately move through it, they will utilize this process to begin to question their beliefs about relationships.

As an example, if Mary is thinking about being single for a couple of years but questions her motives, she may recruit her friend Janet to help her work through this. She may say to Janet, "I am wondering if I really need to be in a relationship at all. I mean, I like Ted, but I sort of feel like I want to spend time by myself. Does that make sense?"

The problem is that most people are plugged into the mass mind system of beliefs, which means that her friend Janet will only be speaking from that level of consciousness. Her reply would most likely be something along the lines of "I think the problem is that Ted is boring. I think when you find the right man, you'll be happy to be in a relationship."

And so, if Mary does not recruit other people, or perhaps someone who is in the awakening process of their consciousness to role-play with her, she will probably break up with Ted and get right back into another relationship. In turn, this new relationship may feel exciting and fun in the beginning, but will wind up the exact same way as the previous one.

This is for two reasons: first, Mary has not addressed the unmet need for solitude within herself. And second, because she has not done any inner work upon herself, she will be projecting the exact same version of herself upon her next partner. Thus "Jim," will turn out to be exactly like "Ted."

For women especially, this belief is one that they have had to fight harder and longer due to all of the societal beliefs that have been inflicted upon them historically. Thus, it is one of the most powerful and liberating things a woman can do for herself when she decides to take time out of relationships. Since it is in direct conflict with our societal, preprogrammed, subconscious beliefs, it takes a certain amount of willpower to move through the subconscious belief barrier and, simultaneously, defend her consciousness against all of the people around who are trying to project this program onto her.

However, the surprising, shocking, extremely liberating, and ultimately empowering feeling of breaking free of this emotional bondage to honor their own needs will be many women's next step in the evolution of their consciousness.

Relationship Energy

A topic of specific interest to me, and about which I had to learn the hard way, was the curious tendency of the "relationship" to impact my professional, work life. What I discovered over the years was that you cannot separate the energy of your relationship from the rest of your life. In fact, my finding, not just for myself, but for every single person whom I've ever worked with, was that your personal relationship has a dramatic impact upon your ability to earn money, tap into your creativity, and perform your job. I found that, time and time again, when someone had an issue with a job, creativity, or money, quite often the underlying issue was not with these items, but was within his or her romantic life.

In fact, this issue was so prolific that I began to realize how deeply it was undermining, literally millions of people on the planet in their efforts at creating more empowering and fulfilling lives for themselves. The underlying subconscious belief that was driving this great dysfunction was "I need another person to complete who I am." Or another way of saying this is "I am not a whole person by myself." This means that the impetus for this dysfunction was coming from a subconscious belief that creates the feeling of "incompleteness" within the individual. The end result is that people were being driven into relationships, no matter what the repercussions were to their personal growth and expansion.

As with anything, the higher the level of conscious development within the individual, the less these subconscious restrictions apply. Conversely, the lower the level of conscious development, the more the individual is at the mercy of his or her subconscious and all of the beliefs held within it. In an intricate and unexpected way, this means that some people will need to create a relationship in order to achieve any meaningful goals within their lives.

Others will be served better by breaking away from this subconscious belief in order to actualize a higher level of consciousness. Of course, examples abound of those individuals who are world level achievers and happily married as well as those individuals who exist at a more base level of consciousness without being in a relationship. However, transcendence is the ultimate key to living a fuller life of freedom, prosperity, and creativity.

For base levels of consciousness, this means that the relationship must be central to everything that they want to do within their lives. Another way of saying this is that, if a person at this level of conscious development wants to be successful within his or her career, then she must make sure that her relationship is doing well. Since people are driven by their subconscious, they will feel a sense of being unfulfilled until they establish a relationship. Even if they are aware of the potential limitations of starting a relationship in the middle of attempting to achieve goals and dreams, they will yet feel compelled to find someone.

Serial Relationships

As previously expressed within this book, my conscious development in this incarnation began at a very base level. In other words, I fit the parameters of someone who was conflicted about his desires and subconscious beliefs. I knew I wanted to achieve larger than life goals one day, but I felt the constant compulsion to be in a relationship. This internal battle, reflected externally as, what some would label "serial monogamy," lasted for almost fifteen years. Such was the power of the subconscious that I would get back into a relationship after only a few months of solitude. As the years went by, I became more aware of the conscious desire to be free of this emotional prison that was compulsively drawing me back into relationships.

Eventually, I arrived at the point where I actually entered into a relationship knowing that I would break up with this person. In other words, I had arrived at a new level of conscious awareness. Although the strong emotional, subconscious patterning had pulled me back into another relationship, I had the conscious awareness that I was not doing what I truly wanted to be doing. After that relationship was over, I was able to purposefully create the space I needed in relative isolation for a number of years, before consciously deciding whether or not I wanted to pursue being in a relationship again.

Money & Relationships & Empowerment

Over the years, working with many individuals, and as a result of my own self-study, I noticed that the "relationship" had a tendency to impact an individual's level of money and empowerment. In fact, I noticed that there was usually a direct correlation between money, empowerment, and the relationship. Now, not only was there a matrix of subconscious beliefs compelling us to be in a relationship, but in turn it also impacted the amount of money we made and the amount of emotional empowerment we felt.

I bore witness to more and more people coming forward who, on the outside, wanted to create the perfect relationship. Simultaneously, though, they were not making the money they wanted, not working in the career field they loved, and often felt helpless to change their life circumstances. The problem was that these people, along with millions of others, were not prioritizing their own growth and development. Instead, they were projecting these unmet needs onto their relationship, fully expecting that the relationship could withstand this burden on its own.

No one told them that, if they put their own unmet needs first, and the relationship second, that their relationship would actually get better. To take it further, no one ever told them that the act of "getting into a relationship" was completely optional.

During these sessions, where I worked with many of the people who wanted to improve their relationships, it came out time and time again that, the real problem was feeling unfulfilled in their lives. These people were coming up against the subconscious belief that fulfillment is supposed to be derived from within the relationship. However, in their hearts, they had a greater yearning to experience more of life and living. So when they projected all of these unmet needs onto the relationship, there was no way that it could withstand the burden. No other person can ever meet another's unmet needs. It is impossible and the basis for much of the dysfunction in the world today. It is the idea that "someone else is responsibility for my happiness."

The answer for these people was never to take some sort of direction or action within the relationship itself. Rather, the answer was virtually almost always to take action within their own lives. This meant that the real answer was pulling the focus of their attention out of the relationship and the other person, and putting that focus back on them. When they did this, there was almost always dramatic improvement. The interesting thing was that, not only was there improvement within each person's own life, but also within the relationship as well. This is due in part because, when that other person, at a subconscious level, begins to feel the absence of all that pressure from you, he starts to respond more positively.

However, this should be viewed as a peripheral, positive side effect, rather than the goal itself. If one were to attempt to utilize this process to "manipulate" the other person into a behavior that was more pleasing, she would be disappointed to find that it did not work. It would be inauthentic and based upon attachment to outcome. Conversely, when you really begin to honor yourself and your unmet needs while being inside of a committed relationship, you simultaneously release attachment to the other person. In turn, that person will feel this 'release' and respond positively.

The ability to consciously decide whether or not you want to be in a relationship is one of the greatest evolutions in your consciousness that you can possibly make. In order to do this, it will mean that you must have taken some time to do the necessary inner work on your emotional body. In turn, this means that you must have been able to create some good boundaries around your alone time and ability to take space for yourself to meditate and just be. In other words, this is one of the greatest challenges and simultaneously one of the greatest rewards that you can ever achieve and reap. Transcending this compulsion and turning it into a conscious, empowering choice will help you in your journey to build authentic power.

14

Shifting Consciousness

The Vedic Seers, ancient Egyptians, Mayans, and Hopi Indians all, collectively, yet separately, predicted massive change during this time period in the history of our world. Thus, many of the indigenous, ancient cultures, which had created some form of mind/body science, were all in tune with the shifting and elevating consciousness of the planet. They were all in tune with the energy of Nature. They could see energy patterns and, as a result, gain the ability to utilize these patterns and waves of energy to the advantage of their cultures.

As an example, the Hopi Indians, as well as some other Native American tribes, understood that there was actually a connection between themselves and the planet. They understood that human consciousness could influence Nature. As a result of this, they were able to utilize collective consciousness to harness the forces of Nature to be able to purposefully create rain when there was a drought. The ancient Egyptians uncovered methods and means of harnessing nature to infuse their bodies with energy from the Sun. The Mayans were able to chart the trajectory of the Earth, and indeed, the entire Galaxy, based upon the science of ancient astronomy. With this, they were even able to predict the future by understanding how different energies from the planets affected the energy of the Earth.

The basic result is that, in a great irony, most of the people who knew when this shift was going to happen and what it meant are gone from the planet. Although many indigenous cultures still exist, of the ancient cultures that were deeply in tune with Nature, the Hopi Indians are one of very few that remain. There are other traditions and cultures that are still in tune with this knowledge, but they remain hidden from mainstream media. This means that, for the most part, we are flying blind in the face of one of the most potentially radical shifts the human species has ever born witness to.

The Speed of Thought

So what does this time period represent? This time period in the history of our planet and, most likely, the entire Universe, represents a powerful acceleration of consciousness. Another way to say this is *we live in a rapid acceleration of conscious development.* Yet another way to say this is that everything is being amplified. The energy that everything is composed of, which is that of *thought* itself, is being sped up.

Now the question is what does *that* mean? I've read many books on the subject and meditated upon it for countless hours, and I've come to an intuitive understanding. I've come to *feel* what this time period means more than to intellectually understand it. My feeling of this time period is that we are all being pushed to take a giant step up in the development of our consciousness as a whole. We are being prompted and prodded to move up the ladder. Although simplistic in its upward direction, the repercussions and ramifications of this are intricate, complex, and far-reaching. The way in which it is affecting individuals, cultures, and nations is profound, yet subtle. Another way of saying this is that the results are extreme, but the effects are difficult to pinpoint. People are beginning to see that massive change is at hand, but they still do not understand how or why.

Why

Since I am a human, incarnate on the planet, living and breathing like you, my understanding is still limited. I have spent a good amount of my life studying and meditating upon this subject and spiritual, conscious evolution in general. It could then be argued, perhaps, that I have a slightly better grasp on this topic than the average person. Yet, I would still only be giving it my best guess.

My best guess is that the Universe actually does have an evolutionary timetable. I believe that this timetable has been programmed in so that we ultimately arrive, one day, back where we started, which is at Oneness. This is the nutshell version of something which is so profound, so complex, and so beyond the ability of human consciousness to begin to even slightly comprehend, that to put words to it is to instantaneously diminish it. When it comes to such things, usually, the best policy is to know that you don't know. However, for argument sake, I submit my belief that there's a Universal timetable upon which all evolution is based. Again, I believe the goal of this timetable is to help those who are ready to accelerate their journey and ultimately move beyond earthly incarnations.

You may be wondering why we would wish to move beyond physical incarnations. Why would we desire to quit coming back to our physical lives and all of the creativity and learning that we can accomplish here? The answer is, again, complex in the least. And so, yet again, I use my best guess to propose that some of us, at a Soul level, are tired of incarnating over and over again. The theory is that we programmed into our life script during this particular incarnation, an awakening code to harness this acceleration of consciousness. In this way, those of us who are ready to can begin to transcend our physical nature and embrace our nonphysical, multidimensional selves.

I hesitate to use the word "ascension" in this context, even though it is the best one-word description of the entire process. For many, it brings up a rather "woo-woo" or metaphysical connotation. In other words, there is an instant and not necessarily positive association and relegation to many terms that are metaphysical, or spiritual in nature. To say that we are "ascending inter-dimensionally" would instantly challenge many readers to the point of a potential loss of interest in the reading. This type of language comes across as metaphysical, philosophical, and without any practical point of reference.

Once a writer starts down this path, what is to stop him from creating an entire philosophy based upon his own fantasies about the world? Or worse, what is to stop an unhealed teacher or philosopher from disseminating his own, unhealed version of the world through his writing?

This is why one needs to own his own truths, own his own theories, and own his own understandings of life when placed in the position of leadership or teaching. Otherwise, even the informed teacher or leader risks creating limitation or false understandings of the Universe and life in general.

And, indeed, there have been many attempts upon the parts of those who are unhealed, to project their version of the world onto the masses. The creation of strict doctrines, laced with pages and pages of beliefs about what we should and should not do, is an example of this. Any book, scripture, or philosophy that attempts to usurp the power of choice is a potential example of unhealed projection. It usually means that it is based upon a fear of loss of control.

Another way of saying this is that if you can get a large group of people to agree upon your rules of life, you can maintain control or power over them as a result. Then you can begin to perpetrate yourself as a living god incarnate, or something very close. It should be noted that this is not an affront to any one piece of writing, or any one type of religion or belief system, but a generalization of how unhealed, fearful people can come to power through the projection of their beliefs.

My theory is that the Universal Time Table is pushing us to move beyond the limitation of all of our subconscious, preprogrammed beliefs. To move beyond the limitation of beliefs is to actualize ultimate, creative freedom. At a deeper level, in theory, we all crave this freedom and strive toward it. We manifest it externally in different ways while internally we all desire the same thing. For those of us who are ready, we can utilize this massive, accelerated wave of energy to push ourselves beyond our previous limitations to realize a power beyond anything we ever conceived possible. At a deeper level, we have grown weary of war, famine, and poverty. We have grown weary of creating our reality out of fear, rather than out of abundance and love. This is the "why" as I have come to understand it to be.

How

To understand how this evolution is occurring within us, we must understand how our emotional energy exists within us. Physicists and biologists inform us now that our emotions have a vibrational signature attached to them. In other words, each emotional range vibrates at a different frequency. Some emotions vibrate at higher frequencies and some at lower frequencies. It also corresponds that the lower the frequency, the more likely the emotion is to feel negative.

Conversely, the higher the frequency of the emotion, the more likely it is to feel positive. As we move through life, due mostly to fear, we suppress some of our emotions and this suppressed emotional energy is usually the emotions that we are fearful of and are dense and heavy in nature. So, it has a lower vibrational frequency to it, which makes it heavier. It has an atomic weight, although extremely difficult to measure.

So, the question is if the frequency of all energy is speeding up, what is the effect of this process upon heavier, lower vibrational energy trapped inside of our bodies? What is the effect of suppressed emotional charges trapped deep inside of us, at a level of consciousness that we are not aware of when in the process of a massive acceleration of the energy of thought? The results of this can be both magnificent as well as disastrous.

As stated previously, often an individual will not be consciously aware of the suppressed emotional energy that is trapped inside of him. Because this energy is actually magnetic or charged, it will draw other people to itself who have this same charge. It is the classic case of "like attracts like," only at a more profound level. When a suppressed emotional charge is held deeply unconsciously, in order to release and integrate it, then it must be triggered by an outside event. This means that the consciousness of the individual will trigger an outside, external event that, in turn, will trigger the suppressed emotional charge within the individual. Often, and as a result of how deeply unconscious the person is of this suppressed emotional charge, he or she will have no idea as to why this event is occurring. And, as previously mentioned, the less developed the consciousness, the more likely the individual will feel like a victim of outside events. However, the more developed the consciousness of the individual, the more likely he or she will be able to make the connection between his or her suppressed emotional charges, and the external events which triggered them.

So, one manifestation of the acceleration of thought upon the consciousness of an individual is the triggering of suppressed emotional charges by seemingly spontaneous and random external events. As this occurs, the individual can utilize this triggering to release the deeply held suppressed emotional charges. In other words, once they are triggered, they are now in your conscious awareness, and you have direct access to them. When this takes place, you have the opportunity to integrate and release this suppressed energy. Deep in the mountains of Tibet, the Buddhist Monks referred to this process as "burning through your karma." It quite simply means allowing all of your suppressed emotions to fully surface and move through you unconditionally. Of course, this is easy to say, however often difficult to engage with. The vast majority of people, upon attempting to engage with this process, will be tempted to identify with their emotional energy as "who I am." The average person believes that she is her emotions and thus, allowing negative emotions to surface for integration gets recapitulated into "facing the darkness of who I really am underneath." As a result of this, a subconscious fear develops about looking deeply within the self for fear of what will be seen.

However, when one can begin to dis-identify with her emotional energy, she can more fully engage with this process. It can be done either way, but becomes easier when you can begin to allow the energy to move through you unimpeded. This profound act, that of total surrender and detachment from your emotions, will allow you to let these suppressed facets of yourself move through you.

When this happens, it is akin to allowing unexpressed fragments of your psyche, which have gone unheeded and unexpressed for your entire lifetime or lifetimes, to fully express themselves and, as a result, fully heal. Each time you are able to authentically engage in this process and allow the emotion to move through you in the form of sadness, anger, or whatever you are feeling, you will heal a part of yourself and integrate it into the whole. If you can do this, then you can harness this time period to its fullest possible potential.

The logical question that many of you may be asking next is "What happens when someone is unable or unwilling to release this energy?" The problem with being in an environment of accelerated energy and holding on to heavy, dense energy inside of your body is that it will have to manifest one way or the other. Since this lower

AUTHENTIC POWER THROUGH SPIRITUALITY

vibrational energy is heavy, dense, and negatively charged, it will not manifest in a positive way. It is theorized that different parts of the body hold different emotions and that, correspondingly, different parts of the body will store negative, suppressed emotional charges. Regardless of what area of the body it is stored in, under accelerated conditions, it will have to come out in one way or the other. This means that sometimes disastrous and seemingly unfortunate events will befall people for no apparent reason.

For the suppressed emotional charges that are either ignored or held onto out of fear, the manifestation may take place in a seemingly more drastic manner. This could mean the sudden appearance of a life-threatening disease such as cancer or even a life-threatening situation. When this occurs under extreme conditions of accelerated energy, it can take one of two directions.

The first direction is that it can appear out of nowhere and, just as suddenly, disappear after only a month or two. Of course, doctors will not be able to logically explain it. In this case, what has occurred is that the emotional charge was able to be released relatively quickly and harmlessly.

The other direction that this can go is deadly. In this case, the individual, at a Soul level, may have made a decision that we are not consciously aware of. At a Soul level, the individual may have decided that, either she is not done learning this lesson, or that she is not prepared to move ahead into the higher vibrations toward which we are all heading.

It can be challenging to think in these terms and perhaps even sound emotionally cold. One could be tempted to think in terms of judgment or worthiness. The reality is that it has little to do with either of these ideas and much more to do with the decision of the individual. If she does not feel prepared for the higher vibrational levels ahead, and usually due to unresolved life issues held as suppressed emotional charges within her still, then she may opt out in order to reincarnate at a level where she can continue working on the issue or issues. This is particularly challenging for those of us who have people in our lives whom we have lost or who may be undergoing this process right now. It can be especially difficult if we know that they could be cured, but for some reason are choosing not to be. You know if this is the case when nothing you do or say will get them to either take your advice or change their mind about their course of action, no matter how seemingly destructive it may seem. To come to terms with this for yourself becomes the highest possible that choice you can make.

For those individuals who want to consciously engage this time period to reap the maximum benefits with the least amount of potential fallout, then utilizing mindfulness and having a daily mind/body practice is the gateway to your freedom. Consciously engaging this rare and powerful time period in the history of the evolution of humanity will yield a much smoother ride and also assist you in awakening your own latent potential. Additionally, in this way, your calmer, more centered presence will become an anchor for others around you who are not as consciously engaged or aware of what is happening.

15

Boundary Creation

An interesting facet concerning this time period in the history of human evolution and, perhaps a ramification of it, is that one may be forced to step back and take stock of his or her life from a higher perspective. In order to do the advanced work upon your consciousness, which is the hallmark of these times, you may need to go back and address your earthbound issues first. One such issue, which many on this path seem to have difficulty with, and yet must be mastered in order to create the space necessary to traverse this path, is boundary creation. For many people, this issue is a constant challenge and source of emotional frustration because of the conflicting subconscious and conscious beliefs that we have about it. So much subconscious complexity plays into the issue that you could almost write an entire book on the subject of creating good boundaries.

False Positive

For instance, many spiritual seekers, who feel as if they are, perhaps, more evolved than they truly are, will try to enact the concept of unconditional love. And, although this state of consciousness does exist, they are nowhere near it. However, they attempt to adapt to this level of consciousness through the philosophical and mentalized ideas about it, regardless. This means that they will adopt the belief that every person is a good person, no matter what. They will also attempt to project this belief through the physical act of giving attention and energy to any and every person they meet. Every homeless person or individual with an ulterior motive, no matter how overtly obvious, will get attention and energy from this individual who is attempting to embody this level of consciousness. In a way, it's a noble gesture. Yet, the impetus of this behavior is usually coming from an unhealed lack of deserving and worthiness issue within the individual.

This means that within this individual's subconscious, there is usually an unhealed emotional pattern or specific emotional charge that leads them to feel, unconsciously, unworthy. In this instance, the attempt to live in unconditional love is actually an attempt to validate her own feeling of a lack of deserving and worthiness. Another way of looking at this is to observe what she is really doing. The individual attempting to adhere to this path is trying to project a sense of worthiness onto people that she, subconsciously, does not feel are worthy. So she is actually trying to heal the world of her own projection of unworthiness. Instead of seeing everyone as already "worthy," she views them as unworthy and needing attention and validation in order to regain that sense of worthiness.

This individual has carved out a rough path for herself when she engages with this mode of unconscious behavior. The reason is because you cannot ever give enough of yourself to instill a sense of deserving and worthiness within another person. As a result of walking this path, the individual will have not created any boundaries around themselves and will wind up being, virtually, completely taken advantage of at every turn. She will likely allow other people to use her to the point of self-detriment in order to feed her own sense of unworthiness. This means that the individual will often take on all of the lower vibrational, negative energy from all of the people she comes into contact with because she does not have any boundaries and will basically let any person bring his own energetic baggage right into her personal space, into her own energy field.

Negative Energy Sponge

Some people will struggle with this issue, taking on more and more lower vibrational energy over time, to the point where they begin to manifest some serious problems. They can take on all kinds of negative energy and manifest diseases or emotional imbalances from this. They will carry on this way, not understanding why their unconditional love approach is not working, and simultaneously refusing to believe there is anything wrong with what they're doing. Eventually, they may hit a wall with this approach when their life does not make any forward progress. They will question their existence and wonder why God is punishing them. *Are they not being unconditionally loving?* Indeed, it is not until they hit the wall with this approach that they may start to feel sufficient motivation to create their first boundaries.

The first thing this person usually feels the compulsion to do, upon making the inevitable energetic crash, is to spend some time alone. Often, in an ironic twist they find that time spent alone yields more healing than they ever gave or received, to or from another person. The individual may then, as a result of feeling better overall, begin to desire more time spent alone. However, in order to do this, they will be forced to communicate this desire to all of the people who are used to getting all of their time and energy. When they do this, unbeknownst to themselves, they will have actually created their very first boundary. They may continue to discover the rewards of honoring and nurturing the "self" through the creation of boundaries and time spent alone.

Eventually, they will heal and return to the world. When they do so, they will be leery of letting just any person through their personal boundaries. They may still wish to see the love in other people, but realize that the highest good is not to "martyrize" themselves by trying to fulfill every person's physical or emotional unmet need. Instead, they may begin walking a more authentic path, which enables them to see the love in others, while simultaneously holding their own space as sacred.

It is not until higher levels of consciousness are reached that people can actualize a state of unconditional love. And when they do come to this radical state of consciousness, they are not engaged in seeking others out to make them feel better. Instead of constantly trying to pour into everyone else's empty cups, they have allowed their cup to become overflowing to the point of being able to energetically nurture anyone around them with their mere presence. This state of being does not require boundary creation because it is so powerful it transmutes any energy around it. Another way of saying this is that, when all you truly see is love, everything becomes love. However, attempting to artificially induce this state of consciousness usually produces a mentalized sense of "false enlightenment." As an identifier of this radical level of consciousness, no one who exists at the level of unconditional love would ever need to tell you so. They are too busy "being" to attempt to convince you of any philosophy or theory about the world.

Creating Space

You may be someone who is either used to supporting friends and family or feels that you should always make yourself available for them. If this is the case, then you may begin to feel conflicted during this time period of rapid acceleration of consciousness. This happens because, at a soul level, we are all being called to start creating personal boundaries around ourselves so that we can begin to honor our inner urgings to nurture and take care of ourselves.

So, one of the primary themes of this time period is battling our inner "should" dialogue, which is an indicator of preprogrammed subconscious beliefs. In this instance, any time you think or feel as if you "should" be doing something for another person, you are coming face to face with a subconscious, preprogrammed belief. It's not that doing things for other people is bad. In fact, often, this is a way in which we demonstrate that we care about each other. It's just that when you are attempting to honor yourself and your personal development, and your inner "should" gets in the way, you are hindering your own personal development.

Further, if your inner "should" makes you run around and constantly put out fires for other people, then it is based upon fear and control and definitely not love. In other words, it can lead to codependency, where you develop an unhealthy relationship with the other person or people. If you feel compelled to help someone out of obligation, then it is often not coming from a place of love, but from a place of fear instead. This means that subconsciously you are fearful of abandonment—either of you abandoning them, or they abandoning you.

Saying "No"

Learning how to say "no" or, to be okay with disappointing another person, can be one of the most liberating things that you do for yourself. Learning how to be okay with the idea that another person might not approve of you or, worse, think that you do not like him or her, can be the gateway to your personal freedom. If this is an issue for you and you desire to evolve your consciousness and utilize this time period to maximize your personal growth, then you will be forced to confront it.

This is usually more difficult for those people who have historically had difficulty creating good boundaries. If you have this kind of challenge, then it often stems from abandonment issues. You do not wish to feel abandoned subconsciously, and so you project this idea and belief onto other people. In turn, this means that you have difficulty with telling people "no" as well as the potential difficulty in standing firm in your resolve. Since abandonment comes hand in hand with lack of worthiness, you may be battling against your own sense of unworthiness as well.

This means that, in essence, you do not feel worthy to create good boundaries around yourself. This may lead you to feel as if you are shutting people out who need your help. The internal dialogue will be that you are not being a good mom, or a good wife, or a good friend, or a good husband.

Although it can happen to both men and women, more women than men have a tendency to suffer from this belief. It has to do with our subconscious, societal, preprogrammed belief that the "woman" or "mom" is supposed to be the "caretaker." Because this belief is still part of our programming, many women, even after empowering themselves to finally get a divorce, still take on the majority of the caretaking for the children. This is in large part, due to the fact that they subconsciously feel guilty for getting the divorce. They feel as if they were the ones to tear the family apart.

Boundaries for Women

There are two parallel realities here. The first is that, when a woman gets a divorce because she is tired of dealing with an inflexible male ego, she is doing herself and her children a great service because the children will now grow up with an empowered feminine presence, instead of a repressed one. The second reality is that women are more in tune with this time period than are most men. This is because we are moving from the mind to the heart, and this is the realm of the Divine Feminine.

Therefore, women will be more prone to feel or sense this time period and desire to use it to free themselves of societal constraints. When this happens, they may become discontent with a husband who is happy to continue on in a dysfunctional relationship. Many women are awakening to the desire for freedom, ranging from mildly oppressive relationships all the way to completely subversive ones. And so another hallmark of this time period is more women filing for divorce than ever before in the history of the world. In turn, however, these brave women must confront all of the subconscious beliefs within themselves, as well as those projected upon them by others who are still plugged into an old, outdated paradigm.

And so, the ultimate boundary creation for many women will be to file for divorce and create their own, separate space, away from their ex-husband and, perhaps, men in general. Or, conversely, to allow themselves to date simply for the sake of dating, without the need for an emotional attachment based upon subconscious, compulsive beliefs. In this instance, they are transcending the belief that they need one, single man to complete who they are.

Instead, by allowing themselves to date casually, they expand their consciousness past that point and ultimately actualize a new level of emotional freedom. If they were to engage in an intimate, committed relationship after this point, it would be one with less emotional attachment and projection, and more openness and freedom. The result is that a woman who has allowed herself to do this will be less likely, once engaged in a committed relationship, to project her unmet emotional needs onto her partner.

Boundaries for Men

Although both men and women can and will benefit from forming boundaries, especially given the times of rapid growth that we are currently in, these boundaries will have a tendency to look differently from each other. For instance, boundaries that many men may have to make and will most likely feel the inner urging to do so, could quite possibly be something along the lines of less time watching the game and drinking beer. For some men, it will start as a quiet, inner question within them that is asking whether or not they really need to watch the game this coming Sunday. For many, this will come across as sacrilege, but for the man who is either in tune with these times, or in the process of becoming in tune with them, he may begin to consider spending that Sunday on a hike in Nature instead. He may feel the desire to spend less time with those who are still deeply engaged with mass mind activities like commercialized sports.

The difficulty for men is the propensity to identify oneself with the mind, which is the realm of the ego. Due to the societal preprogramming that says, "to demonstrate emotion is weak," most men have shut themselves off from their intuitive abilities eons ago. This means that they will not understand where this subtle feeling of discontentment is coming from. They will attempt to intellectually think their way out of their problems instead of allowing their suppressed emotions to surface.

Of course, this will only create more problems for them in that they may attempt to either medicate any feelings of anxiety or depression they are feeling or utilize alcohol to numb the effects altogether. And since this is a time period of massive acceleration, it will only compound the issues due to the fact that these lower, dense, emotional fields need to be integrated. That is, if you attempt to utilize artificial drugs or alcohol to suppress your repressed emotional energy, you will wind up feeling even worse.

The result is that, you will need to take more and more drugs, or drink more and more alcohol in order to continue suppressing your lower vibrational emotions.

Eventually, if you continue attempting to suppress your emotional energy, you will either manifest some form of disease or negative event in your life as a result of this. Since it is actually impossible to indefinitely repress this energy, then it will be forced to come out of you in a more extreme manner. Additionally, the drugs and/or alcohol, in and of itself, have a lower vibrational signature to them. This means that you are adding density to a body that is attempting to shed layers of density already held within it. This will only make you feel worse and prolong the emotional pain that is inevitably experienced during this process.

Of course, I am making large overgeneralizations here. There will be some men who already embody more of the divine feminine energy within them and may actually be feeling repressed by a female partner who has more of the divine masculine energy within her. Thus, in an interesting role reversal, the men in these situations may feel the need to separate themselves from an oppressive female partner. This is much less likely, but there will definitely be some who experience this scenario. And as a result, there will be plenty of women who, being out of touch with their feminine side, will be utilizing drugs or alcohol to repress their lower vibrational, unhealed emotions.

Interestingly, this is an advantage that many gay men have in life already built in, to a point. Gay men, quite often, already have a good balance of both the masculine and feminine energy already instilled within them. It doesn't mean that gay men do not have their fair share of issues, emotionally speaking. It simply means that many gay men already have a good balance between the mental and emotional bodies. All combinations and possibilities exist.

There are, of course, general patterns within the mass mind that have proven to be true. But, within those patterns are exceptions to every rule. The end result is that, if you feel the inner calling to spend time by yourself, then honoring that calling may force you to create new boundaries with the people in your life. Doing this can be challenging, but simultaneously the best thing that you ever did for yourself.

Loving Yourself

Learning to create healthy boundaries is a lot like learning how to love yourself more. So many people confuse self-love with being ego-centric, but the two states of mind are nothing alike. In one instance, the act of creating healthy boundaries, which help to nurture you and enable you to have the energy you need in order to live your life, are providing you with a type of love you cannot get anywhere else. We call this "self-love" because it's the kind of love that needs to come from within you, for yourself.

However, the converse, that of ego-centricity, is when you have begun to worship your own, mind-identified, way of being. In other words, you are not aware of how your actions are affecting other people and/or you simply do not care. There is usually a sense of righteousness that accompanies this state of mind, as if perhaps the world owes you something. People with good boundaries will refuse to do something that is just not good for them, whereas, ego-centric people will attempt to make someone else do it for them, even if it's not good for them. In order to begin creating these boundaries, they will need to become comfortable with the power of their voice and the power of using words to communicate their desires.

Words are powerful, and most people underestimate how utilizing them in a constructive way can positively impact the quality of their lives.

16

The Spoken Word

When it comes to the creation of your reality, historically the sages and masters have said there is a process by which this phenomenon occurs. Some of these teachers have attributed a certain amount of magic or mysticism to the art of turning your words into a physical reality. Indeed, there have been many differing theories around the power of our words when we speak them out loud into the physical universe.

However, in general, most of these ancient teachers have agreed that we vastly underestimate the power our words have in the creation of our reality. They believe further that if we knew how powerful our words truly were, we would hesitate before ever uttering, verbally, a single destructive or negative thought about anyone or anything, ever. So, we must reacquaint ourselves with one of the most basic powers that we've been granted, and in which we all share that has amazing transformative power in our lives.

The general consensus is that manifestation, the act of bringing the nonphysical reality into the physical reality, happens in this way: thoughts, words, and then deeds. We think the thoughts, we speak the words, and then we enact the deeds. In this way, our words become the translators of our thoughts as we turn the nonphysical into the physical.

In the positive, when people have developed their consciousness to the point of a heightened level of awareness, they can direct their thoughts and their words with purpose to create the reality they desire. In the negative, however, when people are not conscious of their thoughts and their words, they will not be aware why their reality is so displeasing to them. More to the point, they will not be conscious of how the words they are speaking are building a reality that they do not wish to experience.

Affirming Your Reality

Affirmations can potentially be powerful because you can use them to supplant your unconscious thought patterns. If you are not at the point, consciously speaking, where you have become aware of your unconscious repetitive thought patterns, then you can begin to verbally insert affirmative phrases into your reality creation. By putting together a sequence of words that represents a reality that you desire to experience, and verbally saying this sequence out loud, you can potentially override the negative thought patterns within your mind.

When you do this, you can create a break in your normal cycle of the thought-word-deed process. By writing down and then verbalizing a phrase of words that you have consciously chosen, you are redirecting the creation of your life into what you want to experience. Another way of saying this is that if you are still working on developing your consciousness, you can begin to take control of your life by verbalizing affirmative phrases that you have purposefully created.

The only drawback to affirmations is also the same drawback that exists when utilizing any of the mind/body science methodologies—attempting to utilize affirmations as a way to save your life and simultaneously hoping for instantaneous results or using the same affirmation over and over again without belief that it will have any positive effects in your life. In other words, many people attempt to utilize affirmations while either not believing in them or having little faith in their ability to effect change.

When you are attempting some form of mind/body exercise and you do not have any faith in its results, then you will often not be one hundred percent invested in the practice of it. This happens when the practitioner basically gives a half-hearted attempt at the exercise in question while simultaneously believing it is of no real benefit. If your internal thought process is, "I'll give it a try," and your emotional state is even slightly pessimistic, then your attempt will be only that, an attempt.

The Outer Can Cultivate the Inner

In order to create positive, effective results with affirmations, you do not need to be a staunch believer in them, but you do need to have some degree of emotional investment. It's like anything worth having or doing in this world, without some form of emotional investment, then you will never achieve it. This is the point where you inevitably come to that age-old question yet again, which is: *"Do I really want to change?"*

Affirmations are like all other mind/body sciences in that, in order to see the changes you desire, you will need to enact some self-discipline within your life. This means that affirmations are a practice, not a temporary fixer. The interesting thing is that by consciously choosing words and phrases that represent the life you really want, you can begin to affect your internal thought processes as well.

As you begin the disciplined practice of utilizing affirmations and phrases that you have consciously chosen, then you will also begin the process of reprogramming your mind simultaneously. Phrases and words, spoken out loud repetitively, have the effect of beginning to sink into your subconscious mind. It's true that your subconscious, although always susceptible to a certain degree, is much less so after you become an adult.

However, repetitive phrases, which are pleasing and create a good feeling within you, have the power over time to reprogram your subconscious mind. In turn, this can have a powerfully positive effect upon your emotional state, which can elevate your vibrational rate. By saying things that are constructive and pleasing to yourself out loud and over time, you will begin to elevate your emotional state and also start to draw more pleasing circumstances into your life.

A question that one might begin to wonder then is: *"Could I become enlightened through the mere act of doing repetitive affirmations?"* It might logically occur to some people that, if you could control your entire reality and supplant all of your negative thoughts with affirmations, could you not also become enlightened through the process? Or, more to the point, if affirmations are so powerful, could they not become the end-all answer to all of my problems?

The first answer is... anything is possible. However, for most of the people who utilize them successfully, affirmations are only one piece of the puzzle. Many people who successfully utilize affirmations also sometimes combine meditation and emotional release work as well. By doing this, they are creating a powerful mind/body routine that addresses all aspects of creating their life consciously the way they want.

What Am I Saying?

In the beginning, it's often more powerful to first become conscious of the words that you are already speaking. In other words, it is often more productive to become aware of and, as a result, remove any self-destructive words or phrases that you may already be using on a daily basis. As you begin to purposefully monitor what you are saying, then you may become aware of how often you are saying things out loud which you do not actually wish to experience.

Self-awareness in this regard often leads you to see that you may not be verbalizing things that are constructive in your life. Even when you are saying negative things about other people, it is still having a negative effect in your own life. It's one thing to have a constructive conversation about the negative behaviors of someone in your circle that leads you to take a physical action to confront the situation. It's quite another to engage in negatively charged gossip about other people, even when seemingly innocent.

As someone who desires creative freedom and the ability to create your life the way you want, this type of behavior is in direct contrast to that which you desire. You cannot have it both ways. You can't be seeking conscious control of your life while also unconsciously verbalizing negative things about the world and the people within it.

So, your first task is becoming aware of what you are saying. At first, you may mistakenly think this is easy enough. However, becoming aware, monitoring, and ultimately bearing witness to yourself takes vigilance. Most of the things that you say that are negatively charged you are not conscious of. It takes effort to first, identify the things, which you say that are negative. Second, it takes the ability to acknowledge that these things are not constructive or serve any productive purpose. Upon identifying potentially negative things that you are verbalizing about the world and the people in it, it's tempting to rationalize some of them.

You could argue, "Well, it's a fact because I saw it in the news!" Or maybe, "Well, Tim IS a jerk!" It's true that you may have read or seen something in the news and there may appear to be some facts surrounding this event. Or, you may have witnessed a coworker treating another person unfairly. However, your negatively charged comments about this will not bring any resolution or any positive effects into your life or anyone else's. In fact, if anything, they will only compound the situation by adding more negative energy to it as well as beginning to entrain your own consciousness to this issue. Further, to continue speaking about this issue will only draw more of it into your life. It will definitely not help or assist you in any way to continue verbalizing the things that you do not like in the world.

Speaking with Purpose

After you have engaged with the process of self-observation and begun to start "thinking before you speak," then you can start inserting your own conscious words and phrases into the creation of your reality. In the beginning, you may want to stick with simple phrases that begin with "I am" because the language that your subconscious mind understands best is first person, present tense. When using "I am," you are speaking the language that will have the greatest chance of sinking into your subconscious mind and which will begin affecting your reality more quickly.

Some sample phrases are "I am healthy," "I am strong," "I am powerful," "I am intelligent," "I am intelligent," "I am vibrant," "I am happy," "I am joyous," "I am free," "I am in abundance," "I am successful," "I am agile," "I am wise," "I am beautiful," "I am compassionate," "I am kind," "I am spiritually connected," and so on. These basic phrases are very powerful in that, upon a certain amount of repetition of them out loud, they will quite often begin to have a positive effect upon the quality of your life.

After you have become comfortable with utilizing these simple affirmative phrases, you can start to add onto them to enhance the benefits. Here are some examples: "I am truly happy," "I am incredibly abundant," "I am vibrantly beautiful," "I am overflowing with abundance," "I am highly intelligent," and so on. In other words, you can begin to make your affirmations more powerful by adding descriptive adjectives as long as you continue to keep them in first person and present tense. For most people, it's good to come up with a few different affirmative phrases that encompass all areas of your life. However, what you do not wish to do is attempt to negate your current reality with an affirmation. So, you would not wish to add in the negative component that you desire changed, into the affirmation itself.

As an example, with the addition of the word "finally," you could completely negate the effects of the affirmation: "I am happy." If you changed it to "I am finally happy," you would be adding in a negative element that suggests it's difficult in your life to feel happy. This could have been the reality previously, but it does not benefit you to add any previous life challenges into your affirmative phrases. Your affirmations need to communicate your current desire in the present tense to your subconscious mind.

So the phrase, "My bills are now paid" may seem to be an agreeable affirmation, but it will actually have the reverse of the desired effect. The subconscious mind does not distinguish between "why" or "why not," "how" or "how not," it only goes on the subject of the affirmation. The subject, in this instance, is bills. Your subconscious mind may translate this into "create more bills." Not only is that statement, but the subject of bills in general, is quite often negatively charged. Now, not only is your subconscious mind beginning to focus upon the creation of bills, but your emotional vibrational rate is lowering. This combination has the potential to create the exact opposite of your original intention.

So, you want to be mindful that you are utilizing affirmations that only communicate to your subconscious mind what you want to experience and which feel good to your emotional body when you say them out loud. If it doesn't feel good to say it, then you need to change it. Of course, this is often an indicator that you may need to engage in emotional integration in order to heal a suppressed emotional charge. However, in the meantime, when utilizing affirmations to purposefully construct your life, only use words and phrases that create a good feeling within you.

Usage and Timing

When using affirmations, it's beneficial to create an implementation strategy as well. It's beneficial to do this because it's easy to either under or over do the usage of them in your life. For example, if you only said one positive phrase, one time a day, it might not have the power to supplant the targeted negative thought process in your subconscious mind.

To use an extreme example, if you are poor and broke and you are attempting to utilize an affirmation such as "I am prosperous in all my ways" to negate your financially destitute reality, it will probably not be enough. In this case, you are probably battling at least one, if not many, limiting subconscious thought processes, all of which you are unconscious of. To say a positive affirmation once a day in this case is like dumping a bucket of water into the lake. It will have very little effect and will not be able to reach any critical mass within your consciousness to begin to sink into your subconscious mind.

Conversely, if you were to engage with the polar opposite, which in the same example could be saying this phrase ten times an hour instead, it might have the same negative result. If you bombard yourself with affirmations, they will lose their power and, on top of that, your subconscious will build up a resistance to them. So, to continue with this example and say, "I am prosperous in all my ways" one hundred and fifty times a day would quite likely negate the intended effects of the affirmation.

Rather, what you would desire to aim for is the middle ground. Saying this phrase once per hour, every hour, would be a great place to start. Or, if you happen to commute to and from work, then saying affirmations to yourself on your way to work in the morning and then again on your way home in the evening, could be effective as well. Saying your affirmations in timed intervals is much better than blurting a bunch of them out once a week and hoping that something amazing will happen in your life. To maximize the benefits, you will want to say them every day, consistently, and indefinitely.

Life Scripting

Once you have begun to get a better understanding of the power of your words and the power that affirmations can have in your life you may wish to attempt to utilize a more advanced form of affirmations, which I refer to as "life scripting." Life scripting is the act of creating and writing down an entire life scenario the exact way you would wish to experience it. When utilizing this process, you adhere to the same rules as stated above: everything is present tense and first person. In other words, you want to continue communicating your desires to your subconscious mind in the way that it will understand and translate into your intended outcome.

A great place to start with life scripting is by thinking about how you would like your intended life to look five years from this moment. Questions you can ask yourself are "Where am I?" "What am I doing?" "Am I working?" "Am I being creative?" "Who am I with?" "What fun activities am I engaged in?" "What kind of car am I driving?" "Do I live in a new house?" "How have I changed my body?" "How does it feel to live the life of my dreams?" "How does it feel to be in such good shape?" "What kind of clothes am I wearing?" "What are the smells associated with this amazing life?" "What are my favorite restaurants in this new life?" "Where do I vacation and how often?" "How much time do I spend with my friends and family now that things are so abundant in my life?" "How satisfying does it feel to feel so fulfilled?"

Asking yourself these questions can help you to expand your consciousness and see that you may not actually know what you will be doing in the future or where you will be doing it. Once you expand your consciousness, you can begin to see the vastness that lies beyond your previously limited patterns of thought. The recommendation here is to think outside the box as much as possible and challenge yourself to come up with a vision that is exciting and fulfilling.

When engaging with this process, you don't want to think in terms of "shoring up" your life. Instead, you want to think so far above and beyond what you previously conceived of that, in essence, the vision you are creating is barely recognizable. This is not to imply that your life needs drastic changing, but is to say that most people have great difficulty in breaking free from their current perspectives. To say it differently, if you did not challenge yourself with this exercise, you would probably not engage anything near your potential. So, try to think in terms of "limitlessness" when you begin to write down the things that you would like to experience.

The basic premise is to create an amazing scenario out of a single day of your new amazing life. By asking yourself the previously mentioned questions, you can begin to piece together this scenario and write down how that day would go for you. Again, when doing so, you will script it as if it is happening in present tense and also by utilizing the first person perspective. Describe your day as you move through it, the people you interact with, the type of work you are doing, or the type of vacation you are on, what the weather is like, what the scenery is like, who you are with, what you are smelling, and how you are feeling. Be as descriptive as you possibly can with this, as the more details you can add, the more it will begin to register in your subconscious mind.

As a reminder, you do not wish to include the solutions to problems since this returns the focus of your subconscious mind to the problem. Instead, create a vision that transcends the need for any solutions because the implication is that you are way beyond the need to solve problems in your life. Instead, you are living a full, abundant, creative, and fulfilling life in your vision.

The way to utilize a life script is to read it out loud to yourself first thing in the morning or last thing in the evening. You do it this way because these are the times of day when your subconscious is more susceptible to taking on programming of any sort. Your thinking mind is less active and your consciousness is more pliable in general during these times. It is recommended that you pick either the morning or the evening, but not both as this may build resistance within your subconscious. It's the same way with affirmations in that too much repetition creates both attachment to outcome and also resistance within your subconscious mind. Thus, in this instance, less is more.

Further, you may wish to skip one day of the week and only read your script to yourself six of the nights or mornings instead. Throughout this process, you may begin to become more attuned to what kind of timing works best for you. Some people are okay to do their affirmations and life scripting more often, while others need to do it less often. If you have strong attachment to outcome, which is to say that you are feeling desperate or near so to create change, then you actually may wish to read your life script less often. This is because reading it more often may actually begin to build resistance if it brings attention to what has "not" happened within your life yet. In the end, these general guidelines will help you with the timing and creation of your affirmations and life script, but ultimately you will need to find out what works best for you.

The words we speak are powerful and have creative potential. When used consciously and purposefully, they have the ability to transform your life into a more pleasing reality. When used unconsciously and without direction, they have the power to keep you ensnared within a vicious circle that is set on "pattern repeat." In order to fully harness the power of your words, it becomes necessary to harness the power of the mind. However, by paying conscious attention to what you are saying and speaking with purposeful intention, then you can begin to entrain your mind into a higher way of thinking. Doing this will only aid you more in your quest to fully actualize yourself and unlock the latent powers within you.

17

Power of the Mind

As previously stated in this book, culturally we have become infatuated with thinking, which has led to the creation of a society of "over-mentalization." What this means is that we have tricked ourselves into believing that we can think our way into or out of any situation. The reality is that we have created a man-made disease, which is that of ceaseless, continuous, never-ending, neurotic thinking. Although it's true that everything in the Universe is made of "thought," we have forgotten that the origin of all solutions lies beyond that of *ordinary* thought. It is beyond the ordinary, day-to-day repetitive thought, where lies our salvation to creating the Utopia that we all secretly dream of.

However, there is man-made, neurotic, compulsive thought, which is what most people identify as "thinking." And then there is a higher level of thought that is received, not created. This level of thinking could be called "non-ordinary" thought; In other words, the kind of thought, which arises from beyond that of ordinary, everyday thinking. The most classic case of this level of thought is the famous physicist Albert Einstein. Einstein was one of the first scientists to admit that he did not *think* of the equations he created. Rather, he received these answers, including the famous E=MC2, while smoking his pipe and relaxing. In fact, he stated that it was when he was completely relaxed that he received this equation and all of the other answers he sought.

The problem is not that we use our minds to think. It's that we mistakenly think that we create solutions with ordinary, linear thinking. When this happens, we become overly identified with the mind as the beginning and end to our life's answers. In fact, it's quite miserable to believe that you must think your way into and out of every situation. This is when we begin to believe that we are at the mercy of the elements. It's because, when you think that, it is entirely up to you to come up with an idea to solve your life's problems, with your linear thinking, you become incapable of seeing the possibilities.

As an example, if you wanted to become wealthy and you studied all of the texts you could find on wealth, investing, and wealth management, and thought that this would make you wealthy, you would be in for a big surprise. When, after years and years of studying these texts and attempting to follow the guidelines, you did not become wealthy, you would get frustrated. You might wonder: *"Why is this not working? I have studied everything there is to know about the creation of wealth, where is my money?"*

The reason you have not become wealthy has little do to with the texts that you have studied and attempted to implement through physical action-steps in your life. Rather, it has to do with the fact that you are attempting to utilize linear thinking, the same level of thinking that got you to where you are can never take you beyond that.

Nonlinear Thinking

Instead of engaging your mind in a linear level thought process, if you really wanted to create wealth, it would be better to study those who have actually done it. Upon doing this, your first conclusion would be that these people think in a completely different way than you do. Your second conclusion would probably be that they do not teach any of this in any textbook you have ever read. Your third conclusion would be there is something very different about their belief system. Thus, when you combine all of these items together, you come to one, unalterable conclusion. This is to say that, they have a different level of consciousness than the average person. Said differently, they are using non-ordinary thought, which can only arise from nonlinear thinking.

In linear terms, where thinking is concerned, the analogy is A+B=C. That is, everything appears to result from taking one step at a time and ultimately arriving, down the road, at the cumulative destination. In this mode of thinking, you are only able to see one direction, which arises directly in front of you. It is a good mode of thinking if you are following directions to build something, learning how to ride a bicycle, or baking a cake.

An example of people who utilize linear thinking would be factory workers on an assembly line. There is no need for imaginative, creative thinking here. In fact, if one were to engage in nonlinear thinking here, it could prove distracting to the job at hand. Thus, when looking at the mechanisms of the world and our technological advancement, you can see that linear thinking is actually necessary. In fact, upon repetition and practice, there is a refinement of hand-eye coordination that yields a higher level of performance in some workers due to a refined motor-neural connection.

However, if you desire to be an innovator in today's world, someone who has a greater impact, then you will need to cultivate the ability to think in non-linear terms. In non-linear thinking, there is the realization that everything exists simultaneously within the nonphysical plane. This means, to borrow from the work of Dr. David Hawkins, that A+B=C is revealed holistically, or simultaneously.

Another way of saying this is that you see a much larger picture when engaged in this level of thinking. In fact, as you engage with this level of mind, you are more apt to begin to see something akin to A+B=C (C+C+C=D). The meaning of this abstract is that you are able to see the end results of culminations of vast quantities of collaborations before any of it has even taken place on the physical plane. This is how innovators are able to come up with ideas that no one else could conceive of: they are utilizing a level of mind that no one else does. To be able to think in these terms requires the ability to transcend the normal, circular patterns of thought that most people are engaged in on a day-to-day basis.

Thought Patterns

The average person has a certain number of thoughts or patterns of thought that repeat within their consciousness on a day-to-day basis and keep them thinking in a relatively small circle. Some spiritualists refer to this as the "karmic circle." Within the karmic circle is a wheel of thought that has a beginning and an end to it, and then repeats. There are a variety of circles that exist for an individual. There is the daily circle of activities that starts and ends the same way as the day before. There is the weekly circle that starts and ends the same way as the previous week. There is the monthly circle, the yearly, and some say a 7-year circle as well. For most people, it is difficult to see beyond their circles of thought. In fact, most people stay trapped within these circles of thinking for their entire lives. Once a comfort zone is achieved, the average person is more apt to settle into his or her various circles, which ultimately culminate in one larger, yet limiting circle that becomes their "life."

To reiterate, there is nothing inherently wrong with this unless, somewhere within your awareness, is the realization that you are unhappy and that you desire more out of life than a "pattern repeat." Even this realization does not yield change until or unless you are able to create some sort of action-step that yields, even a temporary transcendence of this karmic circle. This means that you need something that will break the circle and provide another perspective, even if only for a second.

Often, this is all it takes to create a new, expanded circle of thought, just that one small, tiny instant of transcendence. It can come through a physical event in any number of ways, yet ultimately the impetus for transcendence comes from deep within you, and at an inherently higher level of consciousness. It is an awakening impulse, an impulse to create the catalyst that will cause you to awaken to greater levels of awareness. In this way, you begin to realize that many of the world's top performers are also those individuals who have somehow cultivated a higher level of consciousness—they could not be where they are if their consciousness were engaged in a linear level, small pattern repeat circle of thought.

The question becomes, *"How do I engage in non-linear thought process if I have never done it before?"* The first acknowledgment in this process is that, if you have the desire to learn how to fully harness your mind's abilities, the ability to do so will become available to you. This means that anyone who is passionate about something will create the willpower to discipline themselves to learn how to do it. Harnessing the power of your mind is no different than any other exercise in that it is like a muscle which, when consistently worked, will begin to grow. And, like any muscle, it will need to be consistently worked for a certain amount of time in order to create any lasting effects. This is where ancient mind/body sciences come into play. There are those cultures and traditions that have been able to access higher levels of consciousness for thousands of years. The easiest, yet somehow most challenging thing for most people to do is to learn how to meditate.

18

Meditation

Meditation is another word that is one of the most misunderstood and misused terms that falls within the parameters of spirituality. This is because many people who think they understand it, in fact, have no conception of what meditation really is or why you would want to do it. It did not get this way because people are arrogant and think that they know, but rather because the term has simply been over-used in pop-culture circles over the years to the point of virtual redundancy.

Of course, the most common misconception is that meditation means to "sit down, close the eyes, and not think." It's easy to see why there are many, perhaps millions of people, who believe that they have "tried meditation." It's also easy to see why these same people believe that "meditation did not work for me."

It's like getting into an automobile for the very first time and believing that you should just be able to drive the car. If you only made one attempt, without any instruction, and this one attempt was to be your ultimate conclusion on how useful the ability to drive would be, there would be a lot fewer drivers on the road. Just about anything worth doing in life requires instruction, technique, and practice.

For those people who have tried to sit down, close their eyes, and not think; it is as if they have attempted to learn how to drive a car without putting the key in the ignition. Not much will happen except for a growing sense of frustration. *Why is this not working? I don't get it.* In the same way that it's silly to think of yourself trying to learn how to drive a car without the simple act of putting the key in the ignition, it is equally silly to think that you are going to be able to successfully meditate without any instruction or technique.

It's true that occasionally an individual will emerge who has a natural ability. I've known a few people over the years who, upon the mere act of sitting quietly with the eyes closed, suddenly "connected" if you will, and were able to spontaneously transcend the level of ordinary, linear thinking. However, for most people, including myself, it requires a level of education, instruction, and most definitely a technique. Otherwise, you will attempt meditation and be convinced that it either does not work or that it is not for you.

Techniques

There are at least hundreds and perhaps, *thousands* of techniques when it comes to meditation. However, my personal experience is the less elaborate the technique is, the more effective it will be for the average person. The corollary is that most people do not need a Ferrari 599 to drive from one destination to another. In fact, to add all kinds of bells and whistles onto your meditation technique is to risk mentalization, which creates the opposite of the desired effect. In other words, were one to attempt to mentally "think" her way through a meditation session, she would not be transcending ordinary thought, but yet again, become engaged within it. Thus, the philosophy of "less is more" is a powerful guideline to adhere to when beginning the process of meditation.

The technique that I have found most useful for most of the people whom I have worked with over the years has been the "so-hum" mantra meditation technique. Although I had been meditating for some years before hand, I inadvertently learned about this technique from reading Deepak Chopra's book *The Spontaneous Fulfillment of Desire*. It was the first time that I engaged in the use of a mantra in my meditation practice, and it allowed me the ability to suddenly, effortlessly, transcend ordinary levels of thought.

Until that point I had been trying a variety of techniques, some of which required visualization, some of which required focusing upon a physical point of origin. However, all of these techniques required effort and forced use of the mind. So, rather than disengaging the small mind, they required that you utilize mental energy while attempting to engage with the process of meditation. Thus, I found none of these techniques to be sustainable or offer any lasting, positive results in my life.

However, upon my first attempt at utilizing the so-hum mantra, I realized that it was creating a completely different experience. Instead of the feeling of "forcing" my mind to engage in yet another mental activity, I felt my mind begin to "let go" of extraneous thoughts and emotions. I felt myself begin to authentically detach from my thoughts in a way I had never experienced before. I began to experience an expanded feeling and feel a deeper level within my own mind. Additionally, the feeling of authentic "peace" began to permeate my mind, perhaps for the first time since I was a child. Of course, there are also those rare moments of transcendence that we can experience in our lives that come from physical events other than meditation. They are moments of pure bliss, total nonattachment, or alleviation from all stress that leave us feeling temporarily transcended. These moments are powerful, but often fleeting. They can give us temporary benefits, perhaps even a permanent augmentation in consciousness, but cannot usually be sustained as a "life practice."

Creating Your Practice

Of equal importance and significance to learning the technique of meditation is the process of making it into a life practice. Another way of saying this is that, to meditate occasionally, or perhaps as a passing fad, is to actualize little benefit in your life relative to the radically powerful shift it can have upon you over the course of your lifetime. The difficulty in today's society is the need for continuous, external validation intermingled with the need for instant gratification.

When you combine these two artificial constructs, you often get a person who is trying out meditation and posting images of themselves on Facebook in the act of doing so. After they have received a significant amount of attention, or perhaps no attention at all, they will lose interest. This is because they did not realize any inherent benefit outside of the receiving of external validation in the form of "likes" and "comments" on Facebook. This is also an indicator that the individual is not, himself or herself, fully invested in the art of meditation. Rather, it was something to test out and create some conversation around. Having tried one or two 5-minute sessions, they may even go on to speak about their experiences from the standpoint of an individual who knows about meditation. The reality, of course, is that they are still plugged into mass mind consciousness and have little desire to walk the radical path of becoming self-aware.

This means that the first step to creating your practice is realizing that you are doing this for you, and no one else. The only exception would be if you are motivated to become a better, more solid person for your family, loved ones, or children. Even in this instance, it is still as if you are doing it for yourself as the motivation is coming from an internal place within you. The next thing to attempt to get a grasp on, when in the process of coming to terms with why you want to meditate, is realizing that the benefits are both subtle and cumulative. What this means is that, if you have a strong need for instant gratification, you may wish to tackle this issue first.

Another way of looking at this is if you were to attempt to create a mind/body practice, which is rooted within stillness, you might not last long if you are one who needs to always be doing something. Of course, this is also an indicator that meditation will serve you very well. Instead of being neurotically scattered in a thousand different directions, your mind will become more focused and thus, more effective as a result of consistently meditating.

Working with clients over the years, I have come to realize the importance of coaching people to create a sustainable practice. One of the most important elements of creating a sustainable practice is realizing that the benefits are cumulative. In other words, when you engage in a meditation practice you are actually engaging in the process of gradually cultivating the power of presence within yourself. It's as if you, slowly but surely, are filling a well inside of yourself with positive energy. And, just like any well, initially what you get out of it might not seem like much at all. However, as the well begins to fill, you will simultaneously begin to be able to draw upon it to fulfill your needs. When in the process of cultivating consciousness within yourself through the act of meditation, you will begin to notice that small things are getting better in your life. You begin to notice little things at first, and then later, larger and larger things begin to occur.

However, the problem for many people is that because these benefits appear subtle, they have a tendency to disassociate them from their new practice of meditation. The result is that the average person who started meditating to make her life better will actually stop meditating because her life seems to have "corrected itself." This occurs because the individual does not realize that the reason her life has "corrected itself" is because she has begun the practice of meditation.

You may be tempted to think that this seems obvious; *"How could I not recognize the direct correlation between the fact that I am meditating and the fact that my life has gotten better?"* However, because there is a part of you that resists meditation combined with the fact that the benefits are subtle, the unconscious part of you will begin to feed thoughts into your mind that will throw you off track. The splintered aspects of your psyche which are yet un-integrated, will create the need for instant gratification and attempt to sabotage you.

You may suddenly have the thought "You know, I just don't have time today, I'll meditate tomorrow." Or, "It really doesn't seem like anything is actually happening" or "Everything has gotten a lot better, I just don't have time for this anymore." The thought itself can seem innocent enough, but underlying it is the attempt of your unconsciousness to throw you off track. The parts of yourself that lie hidden within the shadows will start to become active when they sense that you are gaining awareness.

This is where most people will stop their meditation practice. It's mostly because they were not fully committed at the impetus, which means that they are more vulnerable to subconscious sabotage. In fact, the shadow aspects of the psyche barely have to bring any of their power to bear at all in order to throw you off track if you are not fully committed to the process. It's like an alcoholic who is debating the idea of going a day without a drink. They may make it for the majority of the day, until a friend texts them to meet at the bar for a cocktail. Without a solid commitment, coming from their own internal motivation, they will not be able to resist.

There Is No Try

Is it okay to try meditation? Of course, you can try anything. However, in order to make your life really better, you need a solid commitment that comes from within you. Otherwise, it will only be an ineffectual attempt at something that will be relegated as "another thing that did not work." The negative repercussion of this, unfortunately, is that when you do engage with something so profound, but with a low level of commitment, it will be harder to reengage with it at a later time. Due to the fact that our consciousness is geared to put things that do not appear to work into its recycle bin, combined with the fact that the unconscious thrives on keeping you busy thinking in neurotic circles, it is often twice as hard to circle back to an item that you have already relegated as "ineffective." For this reason, I often instruct people not to attempt meditation until they really want to. In this way, you do not risk devaluing something that has the power to radically transform your life in ways that you are currently unable to conceive of.

Baby Steps

The average person is inundated with activities, responsibilities, and daily obligations to the point of making it difficult to carve out any time for your own peace of mind, let alone to have the opportunity to nurture yourself. Thus, when instructing those people who are ready to begin creating a life practice of meditation, I often instruct them to create something that is sustainable under the circumstances.

So, rather than have an individual engage in an hour practice a day, or even the recommended dosage of two 20-minute sessions/day, I tell them to start small and work their way up. In fact, for most of the people I have worked with over the years, I have found that the best starting place is to meditate for 10 minutes a day. This lesser amount of time is quite often vastly more powerful because it is sustainable.

Thus, instead of trying out meditation for a week and quitting, there is a higher degree of likelihood that the individual will be able to sustain the practice indefinitely. Even with those people are ready and willing to begin meditating on a daily basis, I still only recommend 10 minutes a day. This is a way to combat the other sabotage mechanism, which is designed to do the same thing, which I refer to as the "all or nothing" mentality. So even when I have an individual who is really ready to commit, I temper it by instructing them to remain at 10 minutes/day for several weeks. Interestingly, many individuals will insist that they are ready to immediately progress to longer durations. However, these are the same people who will start a 7-day/week workout program, hitting the gym every single day for two weeks solid. Then quit. This mentality is just as detrimental as the one that has you "try out meditation." In both cases, the person will quit within the month, or never even get started.

Thus, in order to bypass many of the self-sabotage mechanisms and internal unconscious hurdles, when one is ready to commit to the process, I have personally found that engaging in 10 minutes/day is the most sustainable starting point for the majority of people. Further, when you perform your meditation practice at the same time every day, and usually upon awakening in the morning, it begins to entrain your subconscious into alignment with your decision to do so. This means that it has the effect of significantly diminishing any internal resistance you might experience throughout the process.

Additionally, starting your meditation upon awakening as the first thing you do in the morning is beneficial because the mind is still relatively inactive. You are less mentally distracted at this time period, so it is easier to still the mind more quickly. Another benefit to starting your meditation, as the first thing you do in the morning, is that it lays the groundwork for a more constructive day. Beginning your day with meditation means there will be more coherence and less static throughout the day—you will feel more centered, less emotionally reactive, and more solution-oriented throughout your entire day.

In order to transcend linear thinking, remove limiting patterns of thought, and begin to actualize a higher level of consciousness, it may be necessary for you to engage in the practice of meditation. If you want to explore learning about the so-hum mantra meditation, then you can visit **www.christopherpinckley.com.**

19

Taking Action

Studying spirituality and pop-culture self-help can be inspiring and help an individual to elevate her life. Usually, this elevation is due to the feeling of being inspired and worthy of living a fulfilling life. When this occurs, the book or teacher has done the person or people an invaluable service. Helping people to feel inspired is one of the most amazing gifts that you can give because this one act alone can radically shift someone's consciousness. It has the power of making people feel worthy and deserving and, as a result, has the potential to catapult them out of the emotional depths of frustration and despair. An inspired person is capable of anything and can accomplish amazing things that lead others to become inspired as well.

However, these same teachings and philosophies can also lead people down an alternate path, one that is extremely detrimental. This detriment is the one that leads people to believe that their lives will spontaneously manifest around them in the exact way that they want, if they merely sit on the couch and visualize it to be so. In other words, the erroneous belief, which many people have adopted as a result of misinterpreting some spiritual teachings, is that little or no action is required in order to create the life that you want.

In order for this event to actually take place, where the individual visually manifests his or her life into being without taking any physical actions at all, he or she would have had to master all life lessons associated with incarnating upon the Earth. The individual would had to have integrated every fragmented aspect of her psyche and transcended the karmic wheel altogether. The nonattachment to outcome at this level of consciousness is so complete, that literally, the thoughts of these extremely rare individuals instantaneously become things. However, you would never know it because they have also completely transcended any need for external validation and, as a result, any need to demonstrate their abilities for any individual or group. At this level, they are more interested in being a conduit for pure, unconditional love to emanate from within them.

Another way of saying this is that these individuals are the living incarnation of the phrase "Be the change." My personal, and impossible to validate, estimation is that this type of person exists on the planet at the ratio of somewhere in the neighborhood of one in one hundred million. At the time of the writing of this book, that would put the number at close to seventy individuals, when based upon the population estimate of the world at around seven billion.

However, for the rest of us, it is still necessary to take physical actions in order to achieve our goals. Each individual is at a different level of the game. Some people have a natural gift for being able to lightly set their intentions mentally within their minds, and then manifest this outcome in the physical rather quickly. In other words, throughout the process of creating something within their lives, they will have taken very few action-steps to actualize their intended outcome. For some of us, it even seems "magical." For most people, however, they are at the level of consciousness that requires massive amounts of physical action in order to achieve their intended outcome. It has to do with your beliefs, the amount of internal resistance you have within you, and level of your attachment to the intended outcome you desire.

You could be very good at your skill but have conflicting beliefs about your worthiness and/or extreme attachment to outcome. What this means is that you will have to work extremely hard to achieve the very first, basic level of success in your life. The more internal resistance you have in the form of subconscious beliefs about your worthiness, as well as attachment to outcome, the harder you will have to work. Of course, for many people, this means that they never fully actualize themselves. They work themselves into the ground attempting to achieve goals that they subconsciously do not believe they are worthy of. For these poor Souls, life will always be a struggle, but ironically, it's because they believe that it is supposed to be. Thus, they subconsciously create a self-fulfilling prophecy of struggle and strife.

The Integral Path

For people who are ready, though, the integral combination of meditation, visualization, and the taking of key action-steps will lead to great success because, by combining all of these facets together, they address every level of the game of success simultaneously. Through meditation, they help to induce an emotionally balanced state of nonattachment. This allows energy to flow more smoothly within their lives as well as more things to seem to "come" to them. Adding visualization to this process begins to entrain the subconscious mind into creating your larger vision. Doing this helps to create an internal guidepost and also recruits the subconscious to bring more of its power to bear on your goals and aspirations. Then, finally, taking the physical action steps will start the engines and get the ball rolling.

Again, for most people, taking physical action steps is entirely necessary in order to create the energy and momentum to achieve any goals. Without this kinetic energy, there is no dynamic magnetism to catalyze the process. So, without taking any action, it's like putting wood in the fire place, pouring some lighter fluid on the wood to help it to catch fire, and then waiting for the wood to begin burning. Without actually igniting the wood, you will be waiting a long time. In the same way, you need to take action steps in order to ignite the energy of your goals. When you do this, it's as if you are breathing "life" into your goals and dreams. Things will begin to happen, doors open, and chance encounters will occur.

Aligning with Your Goals

However, that said, due to the shift and acceleration of consciousness we are now living in, things have changed to a certain degree. As a result of this shift in consciousness, your intentions are now more powerful and you are less able to physically force an outcome. Although physical action-steps will likely always be necessary, it has become more necessary to make sure you are in alignment with your goals than ever before. If you do not love what you are doing, it will be much more difficult to achieve it. Or, to be more blunt, if you are only doing what you do for money and no other reason, you will find it more difficult to continue doing it. Additionally, if you happen to work for yourself, it will have an even greater impact. This is because you are the one who is responsible for generating your own clients, leads, and/or business. In order to do this successfully, you must be in alignment with it. It becomes almost impossible under these conditions for those of you who are running small businesses or are entrepreneurs, to get client leads if you are not excited about what you are doing. You will have to create positive reasons for doing it that are rewarding and fulfilling in order to be able to continue doing it. If you cannot think of reasons you want to do it, it will become harder and harder to do until you just can't do it anymore. And, as a result of these new changes, it will be virtually impossible to achieve it if you actually dislike doing it.

Conversely, under these accelerated conditions, the more you are excited about your goals, dreams, and visions, the more likely you will be able to effortlessly manifest your vision. This means that the more in alignment you are with your goal, the more likely that it will not only manifest, but do so in an effortless manner. Additionally, you will notice that it concurrently takes many less action-steps to achieve this intended outcome. So, although action-steps are still necessary, the more in alignment you are with it, which is to say the more fulfilling and exciting it feels for you, the more likely it will take less action to achieve it. The end result about achieving goals and dreams in our newly emerging world with its augmented level of consciousness is that it is more beneficial to do what you truly want to do in your heart.

20

The Power of Nonattachment

When discussing the subject of goal-achievement in your life, it fits that the next topic to cover is the power of nonattachment. The reason that most people, who have likely taken many thousands of action-steps to achieve their goals, will often find it difficult to achieve these goals is due to the powerful attachment they have created to the outcome. What happens when you are strongly attached to a goal or an outcome in your life and do not have some means of transcendence is that your strong attachment will freeze your goal or intended outcome in space/time. In other words, your unbroken and fixated attention upon this item keeps it exactly where it is in the nonphysical realm, frozen in place.

Another way of saying this is that, on the quantum level, everything exists simultaneously as pure energy. In order to actualize or manifest something out of this energy, one starts by creating a visual image of this thing within their mind. The act of visualizing this item has begun the process of manifesting it in space/time, which happens because your thoughts are actually creative. Before it becomes physical, it will have to take form within the nonphysical.

However, the same power that creates this thing that you want can also keep it from manifesting into your reality. This happens when you want something so badly that it hurts not having it. In this instance, what most people do is to actually freeze this item or event with their powerfully focused attention upon it, in space/time. The reason that it freezes is that your attention has switched from being upon the feeling of desiring the event to the focus upon a feeling of a lack of the event.

Since human consciousness is actually an amplifier and expander itself, to focus your attention upon something is actually to begin to expand it. Human attention is like "water" for your ideas, goals, and dreams. However, what many people end up doing is watering the exact opposite of what they want, which is the lack of it. It's one thing to look forward to an event with anticipation and excitement, which keeps the energy flowing. It's quite another, though, to begin to focus upon why this event has not occurred yet.

In the extreme and left unchecked, this focus upon the lack of what the individual desires to occur within his life, moves from being a strong emotional attachment to becoming an emotional entrenchment. The more strongly the individual is focused upon this event not happening, which he has most likely worked very hard for, the more frozen it becomes in space/time. In fact, without some sort of transcendence or release from his tight mental/emotional grip on this, it will never manifest into a physical reality for them.

This is where the creation of transcendence comes into play. When you are able to transcend your normal, day to day, and quite likely obsessive, compulsive thinking, then you can begin to allow your wanted outcomes in life to manifest. What this means is that, through the vehicle of transcendence, you are able to release your emotional grip on all of the things that have not happened yet. When you do this, all of that stagnant, blocked energy begins to start moving. It's as if you have removed a dam from the river of your life, and everything begins to flow again. Suddenly and spontaneously, things begin to happen.

At first, you may simply notice that many little things are occurring. A phone call from someone you have not talked to in a couple of years, someone you really wanted to talk to. A couple of client leads come in, seemingly out of nowhere, when previously you had not had one for months. An offer to negotiate a business deal from a company you've never even heard of pops up. For someone who has really been wanting a romantic partner and perhaps felt cut off from the world, he or she may suddenly find himself or herself getting more attention from potential love interests.

When energy starts to move for you again, if you are not conscious of what is transpiring, you will relegate this to a seasonal change, marketing strategy, spike in the economy, or your new hairstyle. The unfortunate aspect of this is that you will have completely missed what has created this magic for you. In such an event, where energy has suddenly begun to flow within your life again after a long period of total stagnation, it was because you created some form of transcendence that yielded a state of total nonattachment. In other words, your temporary feeling of complete nonattachment to outcome is what has yielded this sudden influx of energy back into your life.

Temporary Transcendence

The bigger and better question is *"How do I create this feeling of temporary transcendence which yields a state of nonattachment?"* The answers to this question are both simplistic and yet surprising in their ramifications. The first and obvious answer is to engage with the act of meditation. Through the consistent, daily practice of meditation, you can begin to transcend the small, thinking mind. This can yield both a temporary state of nonattachment as well as begin to alter your consciousness to the point where you become less attached to things in general. At this point, it's possible that some of you may be thinking, *"Why would I want to become less attached to the outcomes in my life? It sounds as if you are asking me to "not care" what happens in my life and to the people around me?"* This is, in fact, the opposite of the intended outcome.

Rather, by inducing a state of nonattachment, you are demonstrating how deeply you do care about the world and the people in it. This is because a nonattached person brings infinitely more value to their environment than does a strongly attached person. A nonattached person will not argue, react, or create drama. Further, a nonattached person is able to make grounded, more intelligent decisions as well as to have potentially more access to higher levels of intelligence. However, an attached person, or someone who is strongly attached to outcome, is much more likely to argue, react, and create tension and stress.

Additionally, strong attachment has a tendency to come from an unhealed place within the person. Thus, his or her strong attachment, through an unconscious emotional wound or perceived unmet emotional need, is bringing a much lower energy to the situation. This means that she is attached to this outcome because she feels, unconsciously, as if it is going to fulfill an unmet emotional need inside of her. This also means that she is more concerned with her own needs than the needs of any other person or group with whom she may be interacting during the process. As a result of this then, the more strongly attached the person is, the more likely he or she will be to create the exact opposite of the intended outcome.

Constricted Viewpoint

Another reason that someone who has a strong attachment will often have trouble creating an intended outcome in life is due to the fact that that person sees fewer possibilities in any given situation. The more strongly attached you are to something, the more it appears to you as if what you want to happen needs to do so in an exact, specific way. In fact, the focus of an extremely attached person becomes so narrow that he/she is only able to see one pathway to an objective, to the exclusion of all other possibilities.

As this focus narrows, the desperation and anxiety to make this one outcome occur intensifies. In turn, the intended outcome becomes virtually impossible to achieve. It's important to understand that we are not referring to an individual who is driven and dedicated to achieving his goals. Rather, we are discussing when someone becomes extremely attached to having these goals happen in only one, exact way, and is willing to argue and fight to make it be so.

Since you want to be able to achieve your goals and simultaneously create coherence wherever you go, then you can begin to see why having a means of regular transcendence is so powerful. Through the regular act of meditation, you can and will begin to create a state of nonattachment within you that becomes extremely beneficial to you and everyone you interact with. Of course, there are other means and methods as well; it's just that meditation is the most easily sustainable method. Other ways to create temporary moments of transcendence that result in nonattachment are taking a relaxing vacation, seeing an inspiring movie, going for a hike in the mountains, swimming in the ocean, doing a powerful group workshop, attending a mastermind class, making love, watching a beautiful sunset, having a near-death experience, petting a tiger, traveling to a third world country, and the list is endless.

The important thing to note is that you don't usually engage with most of these activities with the intention of creating a transcendental moment. Rather, you do so because you want to explore or to have fun. Thus, a key element to transcendence and nonattachment is making sure to have fun in your life. In fact, to make sure that your life has occasional moments of pure bliss is essential for your wellbeing. In this way, you do not remain strongly attached to the outcomes in your life that, in turn, lead to your life becoming stagnant.

Consistent Nonattachment

However, many of the above mentioned activities cannot be done on a daily basis. Thus, having some form of mind/body practice that helps you to transcend the "thinking mind" on a daily basis is almost as essential as having fun. That is, it's essential if you desire creative freedom in your life and/or the ability to create your life the way you want it to be. So, it becomes desirable to seek some form of mind/body practice which resonates for you and which you can begin to do every day. Of course, meditation is usually the best idea for most people due to its accessibility. You can do it in your own home, you can do it at the time you like, and you do not need to travel anywhere to attend classes. You can also do it for the amount of time that works best for you although I usually recommend a minimum of ten minutes. Other forms of mind/body exercises include non-mainstream yoga, tai chi, and chi kung or qi gong. Doing any of these mind/body exercises on a daily basis will assist you in your personal development as well as help you to attain a state of nonattachment.

21

Expansion vs. Contraction

Over the years studying spirituality, meditating, and through life experience, I have come to understand and see things slightly differently from most people. One of the things I have come to see is how deeply we, as a species, have become entrained to mass mind programming at a subconscious level. We have become subconsciously programmed to validate our need for instant gratification as if it's not only normal, but that it's also our right to feel this way. We have been programmed to believe that we should have it better, and have it now—that it is our right to do whatever we want to do in this world, no matter what the effects or the cause. In fact, just about every empowering ideology or philosophy that we have come up with has been twisted, to some degree, to perpetuate this incessant drive to consume more and use more.

Now, it's also true that we live in an expanding Universe and that, on a consciousness scale, it is more productive to think in terms of "more" or, expansion vs. contraction. In fact, all of the high level performers in the world think in terms of abundance. They think in terms of creating an abundance of clean air, fresh water, and economic prosperity for all to enjoy. This type of thinking, however, is vastly different from the type of thinking that compels people to feel the need to constantly consume food, resources, and buy needless products. One type of thinking creates opportunities and solves problems. The other type of thinking creates needless waste and allows those in power to continue ruling the world.

In other words, as long as people feel the compulsion to constantly buy and consume, there will always be an opportunity for powerful forces to maintain control. By promoting the sense of righteousness to do whatever we want to do, and combining it with the fear-based need to consume as much as we can, the powerful individuals controlling our world assure their maintenance of that very same control.

Most advertisements that you see on TV are designed to *create* a sense of need within you, not actually fulfill an existing one. Virtually *all* pharmaceutical advertising is designed to infect your consciousness with a false, fear-based need. Many of these billion dollar enterprises actually have teams of sociologists, psychologists, and marketing experts working for them who all have one goal in mind— to entrain your subconscious mind. To say that they are attempting to get you to buy their products is to not come even close to the mark. The goal of these super powers is to entrain your subconscious mind so that you will begin to think in certain, cyclical patterns.

So, getting you to buy their products is only a small part of the equation. Rather, their aim is not simply to get you to buy their products, but to actually get you to depend upon a "system" for your survival. In order to do this, it must appear that the only answer to your salvation, whatever that happens to mean in the moment, lies outside of you. Whether it is your emotional stability, your ability to make money, your ability to walk, your ability to retire, your ability to be able to afford health care, your ability to make the people around you happy, or almost anything you can imagine, if you begin to believe that you need a product or a drug in order to do this, then you will begin to simultaneously feel as if you need this support system to stay in place.

Many pharmaceutical companies represent the most obvious yet insidious example of this form of entrainment. Since all drugs have, as their basis, a temporary relief from symptoms, they are inherently addictive. No addictive additives need even be added in order for the body to begin to think it needs the drug to continue functionality. Whether it is for emotional/psychological stability or for your physical health, once the drug has been introduced into the body as a means to alleviate symptoms, continued usage of the drug becomes an underlying necessity. On the surface, it may seem innocent or even appear life saving. But, the reality is that the drug is most often used as a means to outsource the psychological or physical health of the individual.

Now, instead of facing the issue, one takes the drug. Instead of exercising and eating a healthy diet, one takes the drug. Rarely, if ever, is the drug actually life saving. Even in instances where it appears as if the drug is prolonging life, most often it is doing either one of two things. Either the individual's mental/emotional state has improved because he is actually fighting for his life and/or he has begun exercising and taking care of himself, or the drug actually does not work at all and there's been some subterfuge on the part of the manufacturing companies involved. The meaning here is that it is easier to attempt to treat people with terminally ill diseases and simultaneously rationalize false claims. If the person or people have a life threatening disease, where it appears as if they are destined to die anyway, it is the perfect breeding ground for corruption to occur. Billions of dollars can be allocated in the name of a disease or illness that has no apparent cure or is considered to generally cause death upon diagnosis because if people are most likely destined to die, then the expectations for an actual cure are low.

Concurrently, if the individual does live or the symptoms disappear, then it can easily be accredited to the drug. In fact, it need not even be directly accredited to the usage of drug treatment in order for people to begin to create an emotional association with an increased chance of life with the taking of the drug. In other words, if they die, it was a slim chance anyway. If they live, the drug might have helped. It is very difficult to prove anything definitively and, as a result, the potential for corruption increases.

Third party companies owned by the pharmaceutical companies themselves do many of the statistics that are alluded to in the advertisements you see on TV for pharmaceuticals. The rabbit hole goes about as deep as you can imagine with a combination of corruption, power, greed, and manipulation. The end result is that you need to make a distinction between keeping your consciousness in a state of expansion vs. keeping your consciousness entrained to the mass mind.

Expansion

When you are in a state of expansion of consciousness, you see possibilities. Everything you see becomes a possible solution or answer to a problem. Where someone else sees a rundown housing project, you may look upon it and be able to see a thriving community that has been redesigned with better management. Where another person sees a shortage of water, you see the potential to harness glaciers for enough water to last everyone on the planet another thousand years. Where someone is criticizing the labor policies of a large discount chain like Walmart, you see the potential to create a new company where employees share equity.

When you alter your consciousness to the point where you begin to see things through the eyes of expansion, you see the world so differently that most people will think that you have become delusional. In this way, you begin to see that the real answer is not focusing on all the problems of the world, but instead upon the creation of new solutions for our ever-growing population. All of the highest performers in the world exist in a constant state of expansion that is often personified by a consistent focus upon all things positive to the virtual exclusion of any perceived negativity. In this way, an awareness of the negative things in the world does not designate a focus upon them, but an answer for them.

Contraction

It's a delicate balance, though, and one needs to stay conscious of what he or she is creating. For instance, if you find yourself doing what you are doing solely for money, then you risk ultimately winding up back in a state of contraction. Although there is nothing at all wrong with wanting to make money, the sole focus upon making money will begin to constrict your consciousness, and your view of life will narrow. Soon enough, you'll find that you have become attached to outcome and, as a result, are only able to see one single possibility in front of you at a time. When this happens, you will ultimately wind up in a state of contraction, where everything begins to constrict around you, and ironically as a result, so will your cash flow. The key here is making sure that you always have a good "feeling" about what you are doing to make this money. Always remember to make sure that you never fall into attempting to use force to create an outcome.

When you get into a state of contraction, you know it because there is a certain cynicism that accompanies it. You find yourself often irritable, sometimes depressed, and usually stuck inside of a vicious cycle that repeats daily, weekly, monthly, and even yearly. In this state, you become trapped inside of a cycle that repeats, over and over again, to the point where the only way for you to cope with it is to close yourself off. You may find yourself sleeping more often, drinking alcohol, or taking some form of pharmaceutical or recreational drugs to avoid facing your reality. If this cycle progresses for long enough, then you may begin to start to feel depression setting in. Ultimately, you will spiral downwards, and your reality will constrict around you, becoming tighter and tighter.

Occasionally, an individual will go through a period of contraction that is actually helpful in his own personal growth. He may have just come out of a massive state of expansion, where he was creating, building, and developing his business for over a decade or more. In this case, a state of contraction may be needed to recover his creative energy and give his mind a rest. However, more often than not, contraction occurs simply because the person was not able to see a way out of his daily cycle and, as a result, has become entrenched within a state of contraction.

22

Energy Focusing

One of the greatest ironies in the world is the act of collecting statistical data in order to understand something better. The reason this is so ironic is that, rather than engaging your power to transform consciousness and create your own reality, you are only tapping into the mass mind beliefs about reality at large. Further, because you have limiting beliefs within your consciousness that are mostly subconscious, you will have a propensity to subconsciously seek out and find the exact right statistics to further bolster these limiting beliefs. In other words, all you will really be engaging in is rationalizing your own subconscious beliefs about the world by finding the exact right data to corroborate your internal beliefs about it. And, of course, this is not to mention the greatest irony of all: all of the data that you are engaged in studying and analyzing can only ever be the past ideas and opinions of the people surveyed within them. Even if it were done yesterday, it's still in the past, let alone if it were done five years ago.

Another problem with utilizing statistics to make your decisions is that they are only ever based upon people who were entrained to follow trends. In other words, if Steve Jobs had made the unfortunate choice of basing his decisions upon statistics and trends, our world would look completely different today. There would be no iPhone, no iPad, and no Macintosh or Apple computers—he was an innovator and trendsetter. If you want to have any sort of impact upon the world, you have to think independently of the mass mind system. This means that you must unplug yourself from the Matrix and transcend the normal level of thought.

Another issue that can arise is when people use market research to decide whether or not to follow their passion. Sometimes people will try to get ahead of the game by researching the career that they want to pursue in order to ascertain whether there is a need for it within the market place. The huge problem with this is that you have no idea whether people will want this service or product from you. In other words, when a person pursues what he is authentically passionate about, it often transcends the limits of any market research that you could do on the subject in question.

An example is a friend of mine who set up his personal training business in Venice Beach, California, despite the inordinate number of personal trainers already doing business there. If he had stopped to consider how many personal trainers were already in the area, hungry and looking for clients of their own, he would have made the rational decision to go elsewhere. However, he was blissfully unaware of such problems and excited to set up his business, regardless. In about a year, he had a thriving business with plenty of clients. Now, the question is this: *in an area packed full of personal trainers looking for clients, how did his business do so well within the first year?*

The answer is that he was excited and passionate about what he was up to. He did not stop to analyze data, look at the demographics, or even consider the sheer number of trainers in the area. As a result of this excitement and enthusiasm, he became magnetic to potential clients. Instead of a pessimistic, closed off, calculating personality, he was beaming with positive energy and enthusiasm. In an innocent, almost naïve kind of way, he only saw the positive in the situation around him.

Although he wanted to make money and become successful, he was focused on how much fun he was having and how amazing it was to be doing what he loved in an area he loved. In this way, he was able to create his own reality without and despite any factual, analytical data to the contrary. The thing is—this is not a miraculous occurrence; people do this every day all around the world. It all comes from focusing on both what you love to do and all the positive facets of the world around you. The trick is that, when you focus on what you love to do, it all happens naturally.

You must come to terms with the fact that nothing is static and that, in fact, everything is dynamic. Even your DNA has been found to have a certain "pliability." Scientists have discovered that human consciousness can actually "activate" dormant strands of DNA. Thus, through the power of your mind, you can activate dormant skills and abilities within your mind and your body. This means that we must come to terms with the fact that there is no hard and fast, definitive definition of the "human ability." Yet, we have become obsessed with the boxing and labeling of things to the point where we have begun to cut ourselves off from possibility. When you base your reality on statistics or data, you are cutting yourself off from latent potentials. Your consciousness becomes limited, and doorways to new realities close off within you. Were one to base her entire reality upon statistical analysis, one would begin to see a very limited, narrow, and constrictive version of the world. It is linear thinking in its purest form. It is also how those in power are able to keep the masses subconsciously entrained to mass mind thinking.

Purposeful Focusing

The way out of this entrainment is through making conscious choices about where and how you are going to focus your energy. Instead of watching CNN, FOX News, or Cable TV packed full of news and commercials, which are feeding your consciousness with all of these statistics and data, unplug your consciousness from these items and direct it toward what you want to create. When you begin to free yourself from this neurotic stream of negatively charged data, you can simultaneously begin to get in touch with how you truly want to focus your energy. Since your focus dictates your reality, you want to focus it upon the things that you truly desire to create in your life.

Human consciousness is designed to expand whatever is focused upon; that is, whatever you choose to observe will begin to dominate your consciousness. In essence, this is the Universe in a microcosm—the essence of all creation happens from energy being focused in a specific way and thus expanding upon this same focus. Thus, as you focus your attention upon something, whether it is a desired outcome or not, it will begin to expand within your consciousness and dominate your thinking. In turn, you will begin to create beliefs about the world based upon the ideas and concepts that are constantly dominating your consciousness due to the exclusive focus upon them. If you understand the ramifications here and you desire creative freedom within your life, you now understand how important it is to pay attention to where you focus your attention.

What IS Real?

The argument that some people have when they hear this is "You can't tell me that what I'm seeing is not real." When someone observes something that backs up the statistics they have been analyzing, he feels validated to bolster his belief about these statistics. It's quite common for people to spend time researching statistics to back up their limiting beliefs about the world. At this point, it isn't even market research, but has now become self-validation for a constrictive vision of the world. The trick is that you will always find what you're looking for. Our subconscious will always produce the evidence to back up our beliefs about the world.

On a very basic scale, if you believe the world is an evil place, all you need do is go online and look up evil and you'll get plenty to validate this belief. Conversely, if you believe that we live in Heaven on Earth, you can go online and find mountains of data to support this as well. Whether you have a limited or expansive belief about the world, if you want to find evidence to back it up, you always will.

Another way of saying this is that, if you believe everything you read, see, and hear, you had better surround yourself with people who are living the exact life that you want to live. Otherwise, you'll never make it up until you decide to begin to unplug yourself from mass mind statistics. Again, the way out is to begin to consciously choose what you focus your attention on. Said another way, are you focusing upon the problem or the answer?

23

Creating Authentic Communication

Another sign of our rapidly shifting consciousness is the desire for more authenticity in our marketplace, media, and the people we interact with. While a large majority of people are still entrained into believing most of what they hear and see on the TV news as real, more and more people are beginning to sense that something vital is missing. Many people are no longer as willing to buy into the sensationalized mass mind media-based information that has traditionally been referred to as 'news.' People are waking up to their need for a real connection, one that cannot be found by plugging into a system full of brain numbing commercials and entertainment-based news media. In turn, this is helping to catalyzing people's awareness of the fact that they have an emotional body and that it has its own set of needs.

This newly emerging awareness of this little explored facet of being human is creating the need for a new way of interacting with the world and the people in it. This means that there are now more people who are willing to tell you how they are really feeling vs. saying what they think they are supposed to say. In other words, instead of the neurotic, plastered-on smile that you may have previously received with the verbal response of "Everything is great!" you are now more likely to receive an emotionally honest answer. It's not that there is anything wrong with having everything "be great;" it's simply that we have been covering up our authentic feelings to the point where we have begun to dis-identify with them. In turn, this massive suppression of our unhealed emotional bodies has fueled the epidemic of a "medicated society."

The result is that we have become a neurotic, frozen-smile plastered on, parrot-like society of people who repeat phrases that we think we are supposed to. In the meantime, we quietly suffer in silence because we think that the reason we have emotional pain is because there is something wrong with us. So, we medicate ourselves to the point where we can't feel anymore, hoping that this will help us maintain societal functionality so that we can fit in and lead a "normal, healthy life."

Of course, the reality is that you will build up a tolerance to any medications and, eventually, have to take even more of them to feel emotionally stable. However, to even refer to it as "emotional stability" is a far cry from the reality. Feeling so numb that you are completely unaware of what you are feeling is no way to live and definitely not a sustainable answer. Eventually, the unhealed emotions will have to surface for integration at some point. This means that you can attempt to repress your emotional body with medications, alcohol, and constant activity, but in the end, it will come out, one way or another.

Small Steps

When it comes to creating authentic communication and expression, the best answer is usually to take steps in small increments. To attempt to quit watching all television when you normally watched three hours a day would create a vacuum in your life. You would most likely find yourself bored and perhaps bombarded with unhealed emotions that you have suddenly become aware of. In the same way, if you were taking some sort of antidepressants or anxiety medication, you would not wish to go "cold turkey." Rather, the ideal goal would be to see if you could wean yourself off of them, gradually. Of course, to reiterate, the best first step would be to attempt to integrate ten minutes of daily meditation into your life. In this way, you begin to balance the mental and emotional aspects of yourself before taking any radical steps.

The opportunity here is to create a more natural process where you begin to watch less television and/or start to dose down your meds as a byproduct. In fact, after only one week of daily, ten-minute meditation sessions, you may find that you have watched less TV than normal and perhaps even felt less compulsion to take your meds. In this way, it's entirely possible to rebalance yourself as more of a byproduct of "being present" than from having to physically discipline yourself by denying the things that you previously felt the need for.

Creating Space for Authenticity

Once you have begun to reclaim your center by unplugging from the mass-mind media, you can take steps toward building relationships that allow for deeper, more powerful connections with the people you interact with. Of course, the first relationship that you may need to build is the one with yourself. When you unplug yourself from all of the incessant activities that you were previously using to cover up the way you were feeling, it creates the powerful opportunity to get reacquainted with the "you" that is really you. So, rather than immediately running out and engaging in an overload of social activities, at the risk of finding another way to cover up your emotional body, take time to be with yourself. Again, the first thing you can do is to integrate daily meditation. It may seem redundant at this point, but I bring it up to stress the powerful impact that it will have upon your emotional body and your life in general. You may find that taking some time to read, engage in hobbies that you enjoy, and even rearrange your living space can be extremely rewarding. Instead of spending your time living vicariously through people on TV, you can begin to invest that time in yourself. It may seem trivial to some, but the power of investing this time and energy back in yourself is that it will build your self-esteem as well as help you to feel more empowered. In turn, you will come to feel more solidarity within yourself and gain access to the ability to create authentic communication with others.

Now, after taking time for yourself by nurturing the deeper needs of the soul, you will have more to offer the people you encounter. The enriched, nurtured you that is more present and more enlivened by allowing for exploratory creativity will engage others at a deeper level. Your presence now offers the opportunity for other people to drop their guard and express how they are feeling as well. When this happens, you become a healer with your own power of presence by merely creating a safe environment for another person to authentically express herself. You are now less projective, unconsciously reactive, and think less in terms of "shoulds." More and more, you find people are drawn to you because, at a level of consciousness most people are unaware of, they desire authentic expression and simply do not know it. This means that they may sense this about you but not be able to consciously express why they want to be around you. Your presence has created a window in the present moment where authentic communication can occur without prejudice.

24

The Power of Routine

Although one of the primary goals of this book is to help you transcend linear thinking and, as a result, move beyond the smaller circles of thought within your consciousness, in an ironic twist having a daily routine can help you to expedite this process. Many of the most powerful and innovative thinkers throughout history were known for having a certain set number of repetitive behaviors that they performed on a daily basis. Some were even known for picking out a single outfit that they felt fit their personality, and basically storing six or seven of these same outfits in their closet, one for each day of the week. In this way, they never had to expend any extra energy thinking about what they needed to wear. Similarly, some of the great spiritualists were known for having an unbroken meditation practice that was done every single day, no matter what.

High Level Performers

Today's high-level performers are well aware of the power of creating a daily routine for their mind, body, and soul. As such, were you to get to know any one of them on a personal level, you would find that there is most likely a routine time when they go to sleep, a routine time when they wake up, a daily or weekly routine for their exercise, a daily breakfast routine, a daily meditation routine, a daily clothing routine, and a daily routine for their mental focus. So, despite the fact that their mental focus is often upon the nonlinear aspects of thinking, they have a daily routine that grounds them and makes them more effective. The daily routine helps to keep them operating at optimum efficiency and keeps them on track with their goals.

Additionally, they have disciplined themselves beyond the point where they have to force themselves to engage in their routine. It is simply a given that every item on their daily routine/checklist will get done. If they have two egg whites and a half cup of oatmeal every morning for breakfast, they do not entertain the idea of becoming "bored" with it. This is because they prioritize efficiency and achievement over personal entertainment and pleasure seeking. They are seeking the greater rewards of fulfillment, accomplishment, and contribution that come from playing the long game, rather than the short. This means that they do not live for instant gratification; they live for the fulfillment of making a contribution to society and the rewards that come with it.

When you are able to successfully create, execute, and be consistent with a daily routine, it will be easier to bring all of the un-integrated aspects of your personality into alignment with your goals. This means that once you are beyond the need to *force* yourself to engage in your daily routine, you are less likely to experience any of the emotional highs and lows that can sabotage your ability to achieve your goals. In this way, you are giving yourself a dose of "tough love" that will help you to climb to what may have previously been relegated, unrealistic heights. Conversely, if you have to force yourself to do it every day, or try to find reasons to engage in your daily routine, you have not made the decision to prioritize it. This indicates that you are neither convinced that you have what it takes to achieve your biggest aspirations or that you are worthy of them. It's tricky because this inner resistance can manifest in ways that do not seem related to your worthy and deservingness issues. When it does, it will seem almost as if it's natural and come out of nowhere. In other words, you can suddenly feel tired, depressed, or as if you have a craving of some sort, all of which are subconscious mechanisms designed to throw you off track.

An Innocent Thought

A seemingly innocent thought can occur out of the blue when it's time to do your daily/weekly exercise. The thought tells you that you are tired or that you do not need to exercise every single day. Or, perhaps it says you are not feeling well. Or, when it's time to meditate, you can suddenly find yourself very busy. In this instance, the innocent thought that pops into your head is "I'm just too busy this morning, I'll do it later." Or, the third day on your new diet routine, you can suddenly find that you are craving an alcoholic beverage. The thought here is "just one" or perhaps "it will help me to relax." In every instance, the thought or feeling will seem innocent and unrelated, but in all instances, it is subconscious sabotage.

Actually, a better way to say it would be "surfacing unconsciousness." It is your unhealed, unconscious energy that is feeding you the self-sabotaging thoughts. It has become activated because you are attempting to do things that ultimately disallow it to function. When you create a routine that promotes your health and wellbeing, the unhealed emotional body can become active. It does so because it senses you are going to be engaged in activities that will cut off its sustenance, which is emotional pain. It's a tough pill for many to swallow, but there is a part of you that does not actually want you to succeed and move beyond ordinary consciousness.

This is why creating a solid daily routine is so powerful. You will begin to entrain all of the splintered aspects of your psyche within your subconscious mind to your mission and let them know that you mean business. If you are able to entrain your subconscious to this daily grounding-routine that keeps you healthy in mind, body, and spirit, you can project creating, literally, ten times more in your life than you previously thought possible. The subconscious, through trained repetition, becomes less susceptible to unconscious compulsions. In turn, this means that you will be able to begin achieving goals that you were previously unable to. All of this becomes possible through a self-disciplined, daily routine that addresses the needs of the body, mind, and spirit.

Creating the Routine

The most important facet of a daily routine is to create something that is sustainable. For instance, most people have never meditated. So, to start with even twenty minutes a day could prove to be too much. In this case, it might be easier to begin with ten minutes a day instead. When you do this, which is to say take baby-steps, you increase the likelihood that you will continue doing it for a longer period of time. Of course, if you had never meditated before, then to begin with an hour a day would virtually guarantee that it would not last. In the same way, it is more powerful to create a short, fifteen-minute, daily workout routine as well. The smaller, more sustainable routine is not only physically easier to do on a daily basis, but will also not give your unconscious a foothold to begin to create reasons not to do it. If you begin with durations of time for your exercise and meditation that don't threaten to overwhelm you, then you'll be on your way to a creating a solid, sustainable routine.

The end result is that beginning with short, sustainable increments will yield better results than longer ones at the start. Additionally, having specific times in which you engage in these activities each day will also be helpful. When you engage in an activity at the same time every day, your subconscious mind will take it more seriously. And, to create even more adherence, if you engage with your exercise and meditation first thing in the morning, then you add even more likelihood to potential sustainability because by engaging in routine activities first thing in the morning, you encounter less mental/emotional resistance as your thinking-mind is not as active. In this way, not only do you encounter less resistance, but you also get it all done before you're even into your day.

Conversely, putting these activities towards the end of the day can create more opportunities for subconscious, self-sabotage to occur. It is easier to rationalize being tired, or worn out, or just needing to relax in front of the TV at the end of the day than at the beginning. This is why virtually all of the world's high-level performers will engage with the majority of their routine first thing in the morning. Of course, in order to do this, one must also be ready to wake up earlier than may have previously been comfortable.

For many people, the amount of resistance to making all of these changes borders on the herculean. The idea of changing their entire lifestyle in order to achieve their goals is too overwhelming. The problem is that, unless you make some sort of changes to your life, it will continue to go the exact same way that it has always gone. If you are perfectly happy with this, you needn't make any changes.

However, if you are unhappy with the way your life has gone, you may wish to refer to Einstein's definition of insanity which states: "Insanity: doing the same thing over and over again and expecting different results." The end result is that unless you are already completely self-disciplined, creating a daily routine will help to bring all of the facets of you into alignment with your vision. This saves energy, reduces self-sabotage, and keeps you mentally and emotionally on track.

25

The Integration

Although it could be argued that the goal of this book is to create powerful awakening moments within the consciousness of the reader, it is also of value to create a bridge for you to be able to integrate this knowledge into your daily life and harness the powerful benefits of this integration. In order to do this, you will have to first acknowledge it's a journey rather than a destination. So, rather than thinking you need to arrive somewhere specific with this knowledge, if you shift your mindset to thinking in terms of creating the necessary changes to your lifestyle, then you will be better able to accomplish it. This means that you inherently understand you will be working with long term changes to the way you live your daily life gradually as opposed to radical changes you need to make right now.

Step 1 Acknowledge the Journey

As an example, if you started out trying to learn how to ride a bicycle with the goal of competing in the Iron Man competition, it might dissuade you from ever becoming efficient at riding a bicycle. The goal of becoming a world class expert begins to overshadow the actual process of learning to ride, and you may find yourself becoming frustrated if you are not that good or perhaps giving up due to your perception of the magnitude of the task. This example illustrates the greatest problem most people encounter when it comes to attempting to make changes within their lives. This is the propensity to think in terms of "all or nothing" or, "I need to get it exactly right on the first try." People often think in terms of "perfection" when it comes to the integration of beneficial changes that will enhance their lives in some way. In fact, this is the greatest self sabotage mechanism that exists today, which is that of the "perfectionist" mentality.

The equation goes something like this: perfectionism leads to procrastination and procrastination leads to paralysis; now you're paralyzed. This single, unconscious mechanism is responsible for more failed dreams and pattern repeats than any other. In fact, were most people to overcome this one single sabotage mechanism, their lives would become completely different.

This sabotage mechanism is fueled by the unconscious desire to seek out and maintain the "comfort zone." This means that the feeling of being comfortable can make you more susceptible to giving in to the frustration of not knowing how to do something exactly right and, as a result, never starting it in the first place. However, one needn't worry about breaking free of the comfort zone when simply understanding the power of making small changes to your *lifestyle* as opposed to making radical ones to your *life* will do the trick nicely. This has the effect of removing the pressure and, as a result, the potential stress out of the equation. Understanding this process cannot be overestimated since the average person usually goes about change in this way and will often fall prey to the perfectionist sabotage mechanism. So, Step 1 is to acknowledge that it's a journey, not a destination.

Step 2 Meditation

Now that you understand you are looking for long-term, sustainable changes that will last a lifetime, you can begin taking the necessary steps to do this. In order to begin elevating your consciousness to a higher level and actualizing the profound benefits that accompany doing this, you will need some form of mind/body science. Since, quite likely, you are not an expert at meditation yet, you will need to learn how.

This means that you will refer to my previous link on how to meditate **(http://christopherpinckley.com/blog/ how-to-meditate)** in Chapter 18 first. In fact, as previously stated, creating a daily meditation practice can bring about all of the desired changes and eventually allow you access to higher levels of consciousness by itself.

Meditation can help you to:
- Sleep better
- Feel more peaceful
- Access more of your brain
- Become better at conflict management
- Feel more emotionally balanced
- Become more creative and innovative
- Heal your body
- Appear physiologically younger
- Become less reactive
- Become more loving in everything you do

Since our entire approach is based upon creating consistency through sustainability, your meditation practice should be no different. This means that instead of trying to meditate for hours a day, you can simply start with ten minutes in the morning. You should do this for at least six weeks before you attempt to add in another five minutes. Following this gradual increase in increments will facilitate the transition into making this become a permanent change to your lifestyle.

Step 3 Unplug

After creating your daily meditation practice, you can take the next step, which is to rid your life of any unnecessary mass mind entrainment. This means eliminating things like having the TV on in the background while you work, having the radio on just to have it on, obsessing over the news, getting updates on your phone, spending hours a day on Facebook, incessantly checking emails, monitoring sales or stocks every other second, and any other thing that keeps you plugged into news-based entertainment.

By far the biggest perpetuator of mass-mind entrainment is the programming on regular cable TV. This is where you get bombarded with commercials, news, and shows, all of which are designed to entrain you to become a consumer. Hardly anything you watch on TV is ever designed to help you to become an independent thinker or to elevate your conscious awareness. If anything, it is virtually all the opposite, and to the degree it would alarm you if you knew the extent.

So here are some things to reduce or quit if possible:
- **Having the radio on in the background** (Use music outlets that don't have commercials and which allow you to consciously choose what you listen to.)

- **Taking all news as truth.** Question every single thing that you hear or read in the news; after all, you really have no idea if it's true. (You actually do not know if it's true, but you've been led to believe that it always is—begin to look for alternative means to stay abreast of world level events.)
- **Watching anything news related that you don't absolutely need to** (Most news is actually entertainment based, mind-numbing media to keep you entrained; you don't need it—exceptions would be newsletters that are relevant to your field or any information that is specific to your business.)
- **Phone updates**—you don't actually ever need this. (Get rid of all phone updates, and you'll find that you're just fine, and maybe even feel more peaceful as well.)
- **Watching or listening to any form of media right before bed.** (Turn off all media at least two hours before bed from this day forward, and watch as you sleep better and feel less neurotic.)
- **Being a social media slave.** Take at least one day off every week from emails, social media, and texting (obviously, you have to text your kids or your family members, but reduce this to the best of your ability.)

After doing this for just one week, don't be surprised to find a new sense of peace and ease pervading your life that you didn't realize was missing. Add to this your meditation practice, and you may begin to experience downright bliss. It's amazing the power that simply reducing the amount of mass-mind static will have in your life to make you feel better.

Step 4 Observing Unconsciousness

The next step is to begin to observe yourself throughout the day. What you are looking for are moments when you become unconscious and you react to something compulsively. This means that, in the moment it occurs, you are no longer in control, but your unconscious has taken the wheel. Many of these behaviors are treated as normal in our society due to the fact that the average person is deeply unconscious.

Examples of daily unconsciousness are:
- Becoming irritable or reacting to someone in traffic
- Pointing out a parking place to the driver when you are the passenger (If they didn't ask, then you have gone unconscious; it is a compulsion.)
- Getting irritable with your children when they are playing loudly. (If you become irritable without simply asking them to quiet down or talking to them or creating boundaries, then you have become unconscious.)
- Reacting to something someone says by snapping at them. (Any time you do this, you are becoming unconscious; you are no longer at the wheel of your own life.)
- Getting impatient in line at Starbucks
- The compulsion to say "hi" to someone you don't want to. (If you feel obligated to reactively say "hi" to someone, even when you do not wish to interact with that person, then you are being driven by your unconscious, and you have become unconscious in that moment—this stems from subconscious obligatory beliefs.)

- Spreading news about negative events that you watched on the TV News. (The compulsion to seem important and bolster your own ego through the appearance of being knowledgeable by spreading negative news is deeply unconscious.)
- Thinking that you should go to the doctor and get checked out after seeing an advertisement for the latest pharmaceuticals on TV. (When TV commercials get you to act, then you have become unconscious.)
- Becoming emotional when you see someone else is sad. (You may be thinking that you are empathizing, but in reality, you are making their pain into your own and have become unconscious.)
- Judging the overweight person sitting next to you in the theatre. (All forms of judgment are forms of unconsciousness in this regard; it is even more deeply unconscious if you rationalize it.)
- Finding yourself needing to box and label something so that you can dismiss it. (This means that you will ask many qualifying questions to try to categorize it so that you can then eliminate it from being important and thus return to your comfort zone, which is the realm of the unconscious.)
- Becoming emotional when your child does not do well in sports or cheerleading. (If you are projecting your own unmet needs onto your child, then you have become unconscious.)
- Getting angry when your employees do not execute the plan you laid out for them in the meeting. (Getting angry with other people for not performing something for you is always unconscious.)

- Projecting anger onto rich people for the suffering of the poor people. (The idea that someone else is to blame for the suffering of the earth is always unconscious.)
- Projecting anger onto a political party for your own problems
- Blaming other people for the way you feel or for your life circumstances
- Blaming your parents for your life circumstances
- Suddenly realizing that you are at your destination after driving for 45 minutes. (People often check out when driving; this is going unconscious.)
- Judging anyone by the clothes they are wearing
- Feeling bad about yourself when you see someone whom you perceive to be in better physical shape than yourself
- The compulsive need to cut down all the trees and nature around your property. (When you think you need to eliminate all plant life from your property, you unconsciously feel out of control, so you are attempting to control your environment.)
- Fear of animals
- The compulsion to move in with a romantic interest that you barely know. (You are almost always deeply unconscious when you push to move forward with a romantic interest that you have only just met.)
- Holding your partner accountable for how you feel in any way. (Any time you hold your mate accountable for how you are feeling emotionally, you have become unconscious.)

- The compulsion to buy something that you see someone else has. (Any time you feel the need to keep up or compete with someone else's material possessions, you have become unconscious.)
- The compulsion to project your own sadness and emotions onto someone else who is diagnosed with an illness. (This is not being there for them; this is projecting your own unhealed emotional sadness and victim consciousness onto them. Often you do the person more harm than good when you enter into this state.)

Although these are only a few common examples, the number of ways you can suddenly shift into unconsciousness is limitless. This means that becoming vigilant about any tendencies to do this is a full time job. Step 2 is important— having a daily meditation practice will help you with this process. The more you meditate, the more you will begin to witness yourself becoming unconscious.

The benefits of witnessing your transition into unconsciousness are becoming less reactive, engaging in less self sabotage, creating less negativity with the people around you, having better relationships with your children and spouse, having a more powerful connection with your employees, and bringing more joy into your life. Ultimately, this translates to more success as well as long as it is not focused upon as the intended outcome of the process.

Step 5 Boundary Creation

Your next step is to begin to create healthy boundaries around yourself in order to begin to actualize this new lifestyle. Often, when people begin this journey into the elevation of their own consciousness, they may encounter resistance from some of the people they interact with.

Usually, this resistance comes from their relationships with those individuals that are codependent in nature: this means a relationship which is usually based upon compulsive, unconscious behaviors and out of which you are still getting something. Potential examples are people whom you engage in activities with that you know do not serve your greatest good. Yet, there is a part of you that keeps this relationship going, co-dependently. This is because you are still getting something out of this situation that you are not yet ready to let go of. However, when doing this type of work with your consciousness, you will need to draw boundaries around your time and energy in order to be successful. Otherwise, you will be attempting to float upward in life with a big weight attached to your waist and won't get anywhere.

The types of boundaries that you will need to create:
- **Your life partner**—You will need to have good solid boundaries in place with your wife, husband, girlfriend, boyfriend, fiancé, Life Partner or however you refer to this relationship. This means that you are clear about the time and space you need for yourself to engage in your meditation practice, self-reflection, and your business practice.

  Without this clear boundary, the lines can get blurry and the next thing you know, your daily practice is relegated, putting you right back to where you started. It's important to understand that solid boundaries actually promote a healthier, longer-term relationship. Otherwise, going long periods with unmet needs because you can't get time and space to yourself begins to build hostility and resentment towards your partner.

- **Friends**—With a good friend, this is a conversation that will be light and easy. A really good friend will actually recognize the value and respect you for creating any potential boundaries around activities that are not necessarily of your greatest good. In fact, a good friend may want to join you in supporting these new, life supporting habits.

However, many friends that you have had over the years will be those you met circumstantially. These are friends whom you met partying, gaming, watching the game with, or at work. None of these are inherently bad ways to meet friends except for the fact that, often the way you begin a relationship, is the way it ends. This means the tone is often set upon the energetic environment of the first meeting. It's not to say that good relationships cannot be forged in any of these aforementioned environments; it's simply that the person is not likely to change.

In other words, the girlfriend you enjoy having the cocktail with after work and gossiping with is not likely to support your new positive habits. It's not to say that she won't; it's simply to say that it is unlikely. In this event, you need to be prepared that you may have to temporarily exit this relationship if she is not supportive of your new boundaries. Thus, you may need to start with creating a boundary around the routine activity that you shared together. However, what you may realize is the need for the boundary to evolve into a severance of the relationship itself.

Otherwise, you keep yourself in a state of vulnerability by allowing her influence into your life. This means that, instead of putting the solid boundary in place by firmly saying "no," you have allowed her to feel as if it's okay to call and attempt to cajole you into going out for drinks. I want to emphasize that going out for drinks is not an evil or bad thing by itself. It's simply that when you do not have control over it, it has control over you. This means that you are not in conscious control of your life and, if you desire conscious control, you need to create a solid boundary around these types of behaviors.

- **Rescue Missions**—Many people who are attempting to better themselves often find that, the better they better themselves, the more other people begin to ask for aid and assistance. Those in need of aid are usually relatives, but often friends as well. In the beginning, it almost always seems like a nice thing to do or even seems as if you *should* do it. *After all, you want to be loving and kind, right?*

  However, what may not be immediately recognized is the potential to create a life-draining pattern of unconscious, codependent, and repetitive behavior. This means the person who receives aid will often become dependent upon this aid. It doesn't seem as if it should work this way. It seems as though, if one were to give aid to another who is in need, it should lead to happiness with all parties involved. Yet, the opposite is often created.

  This is because the vast majority of people who seek aid are those who are not in the habit of learning how to help themselves. Of course, there are many terrible situations in the world where people really do need the aid. But these are almost all extreme circumstances, which do not exemplify what we are referring to here. In fact, were one unable to create the proper boundaries, with the people in their immediate circle who were needy, they would never find themselves in a situation where they could be of service to the humanitarian causes globally. So, as much as it might hurt to do, you may need to sever any situation where you are continually coming to someone else's rescue either physically, emotionally, or financially. More alarming is the little known fact that, the more aid you provide, the less likely they will ever be to change.

- **Female Leadership Boundary**—This is one specific about being a woman in the workplace, and even more specifically to being a female leader in the workplace. For women, creating boundaries is vastly more important than for men because women have culturally been denied the right to even create basic boundaries for centuries. Even today, women still have to deal with societal, subconscious, mass-mind programming that says they are somehow 'lesser' in some way.

    Of course, the truth is that, the more female leaders who come into power, the quicker this planet will become an amazing place to be. Thus, in order for women to come into their full power as leaders in the workforce, they need to be in the habit of trusting their own intuition more and more. As they do so, their natural intuitive abilities will come to the forefront and guide them in powerful decision-making practices. Women have had to put up with the unthinkable in the workplace since time immemorial, amongst other things. It's also true that women are more empowered now than ever before and the percent of new female entrepreneurs to start businesses every year is greater than that of new male entrepreneurs. However, women still find themselves having to keep their guards up in the workplace lest one little slip instantly diminishes her authority.

So, for female leaders, the key is in understanding the difference between relevant feedback vs. unsolicited feedback. The boundary to create is not allowing unsolicited feedback from their employees or their executive team. This means that if you didn't ask, they shouldn't be telling you. This does not mean you are not open to feedback; it simply means that you are not allowing unconscious projections to undermine your authority. Far from it, great leaders are open to feedback. It's just that their employees and team respect the fact that there is a time and a place for it.

Step 6 Mirroring

By now you are aware of how you are projecting the different facets of your psyche onto the people around you who are playing them out as character roles in your own personal life movie. The trickiest facets of this are the ones that you are deeply unconscious of. In other words, the more deeply unconscious a part of your psyche is, the less likely you will be able to consciously recognize it being mirrored back to you by another person. A potential indicator of this are the people who we have the most resistance to in life. Ironically, they often offer us the greatest learning lessons about ourselves by showing us a part of our self that we are completely unconscious of.

Here are some questions to ask yourself to bring awareness:

- How am I like this person?
- What am I resisting in him or her?
- What do I dislike about this person?
- In what ways do I perpetrate the same behavior that I dislike in him or her myself?
- If I could learn one thing from him or her, what would it be?

Most people are only reflecting minor aspects of your psyche, but every person around you is reflecting something back to you. Meditating and becoming aware of this vastly overlooked aspect of conscious development will help you to appreciate others more while simultaneously making you more powerful.

Step 7 Ceasing Projection

There are two sides to this coin: your projections and those of others. In the beginning, it is easier to recognize when other people are projecting their ideas onto you. Since this is also a form of entrainment, your job is to become aware of this and begin to deflect it. This means that you want to avoid automatically agreeing with other people's opinions, ideas, and beliefs. It also means to stand firm in your own truth on things that you believe in. It doesn't mean to become rigid and inflexible; it simply means that you are beginning to honor and own your truth on things. When you do this, you also begin to build and develop more trust in your own intuitive abilities as well.

When others project:

- Don't agree with something just to be agreeable; make sure you believe in it.

- Use your voice and speak your truth. (Doing this begins to develop your willpower.)
- Cease the need to ask for opinions and advice (This will cut down on the amount of projection people feel they can get away with giving.)

The other side of the coin is becoming aware of the amount of projection that you participate in yourself. This is much more difficult to become aware of but is part and parcel of the entire fiasco. You are highly likely to be allowing others to project onto you when you are doing it to other people. Of course, most people are not conscious of how the two sides of the coin fit together, but becoming aware of how you are actively engaging in it will help to bring the whole thing to a close. The biggest indicator of projection is recognizing the overt or implied "should." Any time this word comes into play, there is a high degree of likelihood that an unconscious projection is involved. Also interesting is the tendency of people to project ideas and beliefs that they, themselves, are often not adhering to.

To say it another way, when someone insists on telling you how to run a particular aspect of your life, he or she is usually not "walking the walk." Or, another type of projection is the compulsion to make sure everyone else is following the same guidelines in life that he or she felt they had to. In this instance the unconscious message is "If I had to do it, then you have to do it" regardless of what the "it" is.

Here are some types of projections that you may find yourself saying to someone:

- You should get your flu shot. (Actually, it usually starts as a question with an implied "should": "Have you gotten your flu shot yet?")

- You should dress warmer.
- You should start working out.
- You need to watch the news.
- You need to relax.
- You should say "hi" to her/him.
- You should put yourself out there more.
- You should get a new hairstyle.

The point is not that we don't all need an outside perspective from time to time, but rather that we all need to recognize when we are compulsively telling other people what to do or how to live their lives. A good question to ask yourself is this: did they really ask me for my advice? If they did, it is no longer projection. However, if they didn't, then you are probably engaged in the act of projection.

Step 8 Emotional Integration

Once many of the other steps are in place, you can begin to work with your emotional body. It's a good idea to have the other steps in place first because it creates a solid platform for you to begin to do the deeper work on yourself, which always involves the emotional body. Working with this aspect of yourself is one of the most powerful, healing, and rewarding things that you can possibly do. This is because, when your emotional body is unhealed, it controls your life in a negative way. Most of the self-sabotage mechanisms that you may deal with are generated by suppressed emotional charges located within your emotional body.

The best thing about doing this kind of profound, radical work is that you don't really need to go looking for it or searching deep within your psyche. Most of the time, the issues in your emotional body will make themselves known to you through the emotions that you are feeling. All you have to do is be ready and willing to do the profound work of permanently integrating these suppressed emotional charges when they arise in the moment.

Emotional Integration

1. Recognize that you are feeling a negative emotion; anxiety, depression, sadness, grief, anger, resentment, frustration, jealousy, envy.
2. Find a place where you can be by yourself for five minutes (office cubicle, meeting room, bathroom, living room, your car, etc.)
3. Close your eyes and take a deep breath, relax as best as you can in the space you found.
4. Now, see if you can fully allow this emotional feeling to come up to the surface of your awareness. Another way of saying this is that, most likely you are doing what everyone does, which is to resist fully feeling it, as it tends to be disruptive or make you feel as if you are not in control. In turn, this creates anxiety when we try to repress our feelings of frustration, anger, jealousy, envy, sadness, and depression.
5. Now see if you can fully relax into it, allow every cell of your body to relax into and surrender to the emotion. Allow your body to fully feel it while, in the background, you witness this transpiring.
6. Let your body organically express whatever the emotion is fully. Let it run its course. This means that you may cry, feel anger, or whatever comes up. Your job is to allow it to just come out in its own way.
7. Now, see if you can let it go.
8. Now, take a deep breath, shake it off, and open your eyes.

9. Do this any time you feel negative emotion welling up within you or you feel triggered by a person or event in your life. In this way, you will begin to integrate all of the suppressed emotional charges within you that generate the self defeating behaviors that keep you in pattern repeat aspects of your life.

10. Repeat as necessary.

It's interesting that one of the most profound things we can do as humans is to simply allow our unexpressed emotions to run their course. With enough people practicing this one exercise, you would bear witness to a massive radical shift in consciousness on the planet.

Step 9 Speaking with Power

Now that your emotional body is being taken care of, you can begin to monitor and choose your words with purpose. This means that, not only will you begin to watch how you are wording things and what you are saying out loud to the Universe, but you also will begin to speak with purpose and clarity about the reality that you desire to create. What do you want to create? These are the terms with which you want to begin thinking when it comes to the words you are using to communicate with others and in general. Most people grossly underestimate the power of their words, but this is not an option for the conscious seeker. Rather, your mission is to begin to choose your words with care, knowing that they are laying the foundation for the life you live.

Power Speaking:
- Begin to speak about the outcomes you would like to see transpire in the world instead of the ones you don't want to see.

- Begin to speak about the outcomes you would like to see transpire in your own life instead of the ones you don't want to see.
- Begin to speak about the outcomes in the lives of the people in your life that you would like to see instead of the ones you don't want to see.
- When you find yourself speaking negatively about other people, places, or things ask yourself: Is there value here? Sometimes there is value in acknowledging a situation that needs to be corrected or worked on. However, more often than not, the negativity only spreads with discussion of the topic in a negative way.
- Start redirecting yourself into the positive facets of the subject matter. Ask yourself, how could I make this better?
- Avoid conversations with people who complain about the "state of the world." These conversations rarely actually produce any positive change, but instead feed the unhealed collective emotional body of the world and exacerbate the problem.
- Start your day with positive affirmations about the good you would like to do in the world.

Step 10 Creating Your Routine

Now you are finally ready to put the whole thing together into a daily routine. You don't need to get overwhelmed by this; remember, the idea is the journey, not the destination. This means that your job is to gradually build a routine around these concepts that creates a lifestyle, not a sudden, drastic change in your life. However, the willingness to do this will yield powerful changes over time that will help you to live a more deeply fulfilling life. Additionally, you will be more likely to be able to create powerful changes on the planet by integrating these changes into your life.

Although ultimately you will be creating a routine that works best for you, I will give you a sample routine below that you can use as a potential guideline to help you. Remember, in the beginning "less is more" which means, start small and build your foundation through consistency. It is 1,000 times more powerful to create an easy routine that lasts a lifetime than a difficult routine that lasts one month. Make sense?

Sample Daily Power Routine

1. Ten minutes of meditation in the morning, first thing.
2. Follow with visualizing your day, as you would like it to be.
3. Read your personal mission statement in life out loud to yourself; it could be a sentence, a paragraph, or a page in length.
4. Engage with a mini-exercise routine that takes only 5-10 minutes, but gets the heart rate up a little and the blood flowing in your body, thus elevating your metabolism.
5. Be mindful of yourself throughout the day, being careful to watch for when you "check out" or go unconscious.
6. Watch out for times when you are projecting your truth onto someone else or when someone else is trying to project theirs onto you.
7. Pay attention to how each person is mirroring a part of you back to you throughout the day.
8. If a negative emotion arises within you, either spontaneously or through a triggered event, take a minute to integrate it.

9. Redirect yourself into the positive when you realize that you are speaking negatively about a situation in a way that is not productive.
10. When you come home, take a moment to just be instead of plugging into the TV or news.
11. Be sure to turn off all forms of media at least two hours before bed.
12. Take a minute to close your eyes and breathe before going to sleep.

This is only a sample routine, but you can get an idea of the structure. Most people I have worked with over the years eventually create their own routines that work best for them. For instance, some people enjoy meditating in the morning, but some people find it better to meditate in the evening. Some people enjoy doing a little exercise every day and others will do longer periods of exercise, but for fewer days of the week. Some people will work with all of the concepts on a daily basis, while others will pick days of the week to work on each one individually.

Regardless of how you choose to put it together, creating your daily routine is important because it is the vehicle through which you will begin to elevate your consciousness. Everything amazing that has ever been created has been done through some form of organized structure. In order to begin to harness your energy and build authentic power within yourself, you will need to think in terms of structure. Starting by developing your own routine will lay the foundation for this structure to build in your life. In turn, you can begin to build authentic power and completely transform the quality of your life.

This is your journey.

To contact me directly, or to get on the newsletter email list: **www.christopherpinckley.com**

www.ingramcontent.com/pod-product-compliance
Lightning Source LLC
Chambersburg PA
CBHW050113280326
41933CB00010B/1075